If I'd Only Known...
Sexual Abuse in or out of the Family:
A Guide to Prevention

Copyright © Dorothy Neddermeyer, 2000

Published by
Millennial Mind Publishing™
http://www.american-book.com
Salt Lake City, Utah,

Printed in the United States of America
12 10 9 8 7 6 5 4 3 2 1

Cover Design, Jana Rade, jrade@impactstudiosonline.com

Library of Congress Cataloging-in-Publication Data is available upon request.

ISBN 1-930586-16-7

If I'd Only Known...

Sexual Abuse in or out of the Family:
A Guide to Prevention

By Dorothy M. Neddermeyer, LCSW

This book is dedicated to Teresa Carbone, Patricia Aufiero, Danielle Yeomans, Kathy, Patricia H., Debra, TJ Howell, Joyce Meyers, Johnnie Banks, M. O'Keefe, Sr., Carmine, Steven, Merle Graf Gaiser Fox, Daisy, Antonette Burion-Nolfi, Joan Rozella and the many other sexual abuse or incest survivors who are healing or have healed their trauma. These people are to be commended for their courage to say, "I was sexually abused, but I am not ashamed. I did not do anything wrong."

The strength and courage to heal sexual abuse/incest trauma is unparalleled. No other trauma leaves an injury as pervasive, profound and extensive.

A special dedication to Kimberly Swearingen (mother of five, three boys and two girls), who implored and encouraged me to write this book.

Jacqueline and Shaun deserve honorary dedication as an extraordinarily wonderful daughter and son, who have been especially supportive. What would I have done without you? You have taught and inspired me to be the person, mother and therapist I am today. Thank you for being the wonderful people you are and for choosing me to be your mother.

- Dorothy M. Neddermeyer

Foreword

Over the last several years many informative and educational books have been written about incest and child sexual abuse. That this heretofore taboo subject is being addressed is of the utmost importance to enlighten society regarding this heinous crime against our innocent children. While this terrible crime has been expounded on extensively, little has been offered in the way of preventing it.

Prevention has eluded all of society, even passionate and committed prevention advocates, such as myself, because we concentrated our efforts entirely on repairing the damage. As the president and founder of MOTHERS AGAINST SEXUAL ABUSE (MASA), I see the carnage of lives on a daily basis. However, I have been too busy dealing with the ill effects of abuse to effectively consider prevention.

Dorothy M. Neddermeyer has taken a bold stance by writing, *If I'd Only Known... Sexual Abuse in or out of the Family: A Guide to Prevention.* Without vilifying the perpetrator, she has revealed the most frequent abuser within the family and the cruel realities of childhood sexual and physical abuse. She offers practical, clear, concise solutions for prevention.

Child sexual abuse is the greatest hidden epidemic in the world. According to current U.S. statistics, as high as 62 percent of females and 31 percent of males will be sexually violated before age 18. According to a telephone survey taken randomly across the U.S. in 1997 by the National Institute of Mental Health of Harvard Medical School, 67 percent of America's parents hit their child at least once a week. Twenty-three states allow corporal punishment in public schools. Ms. Neddermeyer reveals detailed, compelling information indicating the fact that physical violation of a child's body can be experienced as sexual or often leaves him or her vulnerable to sexual abuse. If a disease affected our children in these enormous numbers we would declare a national emergency. Monies for research to find a cure would be made available immediately. Sadly, this is not a platform that you will find popular with politicians or a topic of conversation at a social gathering. Americans have always taken the stance that what happens in the family is a "family matter." Family values are the platform for many elected officials without looking at the real issue, "What constitutes a family?"

Marilyn Van Derbur Atler, a former Miss America and a friend of mine, defines INCEST as, "The worst six-letter word in the English language." Marilyn's father molested her from the age of 5 until the age of 18. From one of the most prominent families in America, Marilyn was a brave pioneer by speaking about sexual abuse, thus prompting others to come forward. Marilyn's experience also shattered the myth that incest only occurred in the lower socio-economic levels of society. Marilyn Van Derbur Atler's courage opened the door to healing and hope for survivors all over the world.

While most experts would agree that no child is a match for a predatory adult, this does not mean that we can ignore the facts or neglect to empower our children with the best tools possible. Empowering our children with such knowledge as to TELL MOMMY AND DADDY EVERYTHING--NO SECRETS, or teaching them to protest when any touch doesn't feel right makes perfect sense. Ms. Neddermeyer urges these skills need to be taught as soon as the child begins to talk.

No adult has the right to violate a child. Children are our greatest natural resource. Every child has the right to grow up and reach his or her greatest potential. It is our responsibility, as the custodians of the future, to make our children's world safe. We all share the responsibility of protecting our children who are the future of this great world. We cannot afford to have these future leaders devoid of spiritual, mental, emotional and physical integrity.

In the final analysis, we have a responsibility to protect our children so they can reach their greatest potential, free of adults who may exploit and alter that divine gift—potential.

Claire R. Reeves
President/Founder/Chief Executive Officer
Mothers Against Sexual Abuse, MASA

Contents

All of the stories quoted in this book are derived from real individuals whom I interviewed with their consent. In order to protect their privacy, however, all names have been changed, except when permission was granted. Identifying details have been altered or omitted. Any similarity to other survivor stories is a coincidence. However, this similarity confirms the reality: perpetrators of sexual abuse and incest have an identifiable modus operandi not unlike many other perpetrators of crimes.

Introduction

An ordinary, busy day had come to an end. After saying my prayers I rolled over in bed and dozed off to find a dream when the phone rang.

"Hello," I answered groggily. It was my friend, Sherry.

"Sorry to wake you," she exclaimed.

Instinctively, I knew something was wrong.

"What is going on?" I hoped it wasn't something terrible.

"I don't want to upset you, but I need to talk to someone. John [her 3-year-old grandson] was sexually abused today," she blurted out.

Horrified, I bolted upright in bed, my mind racing. How could this happen? I knew her daughter; she was a responsible, conscientious mother. She never left her son with anyone except family members or close friends. I informed her I was wide-awake and that we could talk as long as she needed.

The ensuing story was unbelievable, yet I had heard similar stories many times before, not from the grandmother of the victim, but from the victim. You will read about the incident in this book. After hanging up the phone I felt more helpless than ever before. There was nothing I could do except to console my friend and advise her, "what to do after the fact." The disturbing thought that if this mother could not protect her child, then what mother could--she had done everything right--was seared in my mind. An overwhelming sense of frustration and rage came over me.

The thought of writing a book was the furthest thing from my mind. Weeks later while talking to Kim, the mother of the victim, she implored, "You need to write a book, telling parents how to protect their children. If only I had known ...that JM would potentially abuse other children because he was sexually abused, I would never have let John play in the backyard alone with him." She was right, if only parents knew the fact that sexual abuse is perpetrated, "anywhere, anytime, and by someone you least expect," they could be helpful in preventing abuse or stopping abuse from occurring more than once by the same perpetrator. John was more fortunate than most victims of sexual abuse; his mother had taught him the "NO SECRETS" rule and "your body is yours." Therefore, he told his mother immediately and she contacted professionals to help her reconcile John's traumatic experience.

The idea of writing a book overwhelmed me. I decided that writing a feature article for a magazine would be the most expedient and effective way to help parents. The article defined sexual abuse and the six principals to "abuse-proof" your child beginning from birth. The 20-plus magazines I contacted did not accept it. Since the

Editor-in-Chief does not reveal reasons as to why the article was not accepted, I do not know if it was rejected because of the explicit topic or the quality of writing.

There are several books regarding prevention of childhood sexual abuse; however, these books fail to arm parents with information to prevent abuse by the most frequent abusers--family members. Statistics reveal that 80 percent of children are abused by a family member. Tragically, because a plethora of books promote prevention of abuse from perpetrators outside the family, we understandably believe we do not need to be concerned about someone in the family. Additionally, the majority of news media reports depict sensationalized stories of abuse perpetrated by a stranger. Therefore, we collectively breathe a sigh of relief, believing that it would not happen in our family. Not so, as my friend's daughter, Kim, knows. It happens in the best of families, when and by whom you least expect.

Being a determined woman of conviction, and knowing that parents were not being given accurate information or guidance to protect their children from this horrible crime, I decided to write a book. Thus, *Protect Your Child from Sexual Abuse Perpetrators* was published in August 1995. Now, after several years of speaking on the topic, hearing more stories, and obtaining feedback from parents who had used the book, I realized the book needed to be expanded.

This groundbreaking, revised book is short, easy-to-read, practical, and hands-on with checklists and direct advice, including step-by-step instructions to "abuse proof" your child. This book includes:

- Six principles to "abuse-proof" your child beginning from birth.
- Compelling reasons to avoid spanking your child.
- Detailed profiles of perpetrators.
- Checklist for identifying potential perpetrators who have contact with your child, such as coaches, scout leaders, recreation leaders, teachers, clergy, and other trusted adults.
- What to do if your child alludes to or states they were sexually abused.
- Sexual Abuse or Incest Prevention Checklist.
- Tips to Choose the Right Daycare Facility.
- Interview Questions for Childcare Workers.
- Survival Skills for Independence.

One mother, herself a sexual abuse survivor, has used the protection methods herein and has graciously written about her experience:

"I am a healed sexual abuse survivor, a wife and mother. I knew I would need support and guidance as a mother, because the parenting I had experienced left me with 'what not to do.' My childhood was filled with fear and anxiety, due to being spanked and sexually abused, certainly not a model to base my parenting on. Dorothy Neddermeyer's book, *Protect Your Child from Sexual Abuse Perpetrators* has played a major role in my being the effective parent I am today. This book is clear, concise and informative in describing effective parenting skills as well as what sexual abuse and incest is, how perpetrators operate, and an instructive how-to guide in the techniques to protect your child from this horrible crime... I am pleased about all the tips, checklists, and additional information that is included in the revised edition--*If I'd Only Known... Sexual Abuse in or out of the Family: A Guide to Prevention* --I am especially pleased about the compelling reasons to avoid spanking children, and 'Survival Skills for Independence.'

"My story is typical of Dorothy's descripstions of how sexual abuse is perpetrated. My father molested me from age 5 or under (the exact age is not clear to me) until age 16. I never felt strong enough to confront him to stop. He stopped when I started dating. He also abused other family members. My mother claimed to have not been suspicious. 'I trusted him,' she stated in a matter-of-fact tone. I urge parents, especially mothers, to heed the principles of 'Appropriate Suspicion.' Although mothers can't be everywhere and see everything at all times, a child will display the signs of sexual abuse immediately afterwards. Armed with the 'Appropriate Suspicion' principles and knowledge of the signs of sexual abuse as outlined in this book, a mother can quickly discern 'something is wrong' and make sure the issue is resolved. How my mother did not know the abuse was going on, I do not know. When I was about 12 years old, my father, on more than one occasion, instructed me, in front of her, to come to the den and the abuse occurred while she was in the next room. Also, around that time, he began coming into my room two or three nights a week after my siblings and I had gone to bed or early in the morning if he had been out on a fire call. He was a volunteer fireman. I dreaded hearing the fire siren.

"My son was born during my recovery. When he was 3 months old, I confronted my father about what he had done. Although, he didn't deny it, he was unwilling to seek recovery for himself. Knowing how quickly and easily someone can sexually abuse a child, I am unwilling to allow my children to be around their grandfather. I am not willing to take the chance that while holding my son or daughter that he might reach under their diaper or pants and touch their genital area. It only takes a split second for someone to abuse a child even while the parent is in the same room. I would be constantly thinking, 'Would he do something if I looked away?' My son, age 6, has not seen his grandfather since he was 3 months old and my daughter, age 2½, has never seen her grandfather. I know my children's lives are more peaceful and uncomplicated because they are protected from the tension and fear I would have if I allowed him to be around them. Would he abuse them? I don't know. I am not willing to take that risk. Furthermore, I don't want to put my children through the ordeal of my fear and related tension.

"I also chose to protect the children in my extended family when I sent a letter to my relatives informing them of my father molesting me. Now he is excluded from all family events that involve children. Dorothy's book validates what I know to be true about child molesters (having been a victim myself) and thus, I have the courage to exclude my father from my children's lives.

"In addition to protecting my children from a known perpetrator, I also protect my children from unknown perpetrators by using the techniques Dorothy describes in this book. Of all the parenting books I have read, this is the only book that specifically tells parents what to say to their child, and how to teach their child to inform you so that you can protect them.

"The technique I use most often is teaching my child, 'Your body is beautiful, perfect, private and special.' I told my son this story the first time when he was 2. All of the following information comes from this book. Sometimes I tell the story at bath time by saying, 'Your body is beautiful, perfect, private and special.' I go on to say how, 'No one has the right to touch your body in ways that are uncomfortable or in ways that hurt, not even Mommy, Daddy or a friend.' Then I review his body parts and tell him that if anyone touches him in his private parts, he is to say, 'Don't touch me,' in a loud voice. The last part of my talk is that, 'We have the, "Tell Mommy and Daddy Everything--No Secrets Rule."' When he was 4, he asked me what I would do to the person who tried to touch him in his private parts. I told him that I will call the police. Sometimes when I say that, he giggles. I think he giggles because it empowers him to know that I will take care of him.

"Some of the most poignant aspects of Dorothy's book for me are 'teaching your child good body image' and 'your body is yours.' She emphasizes things that, as a parent, I would not have thought of doing for my child. I would never have thought to knock before I entered their room; to only kiss my child on the cheeks—not on the lips; that if my child resists a hug to let him or her be; and to avoid forcing a child to give a kiss or hug to anyone, including their grandparents. These subtleties of respect are usually reserved for adults, yet what she says makes so much sense. This demonstration of respect supports the child's self-esteem and teaches a child good self-awareness, and that they can command respect.

"Just recently, due to Megan's Law in New Jersey, a flyer was circulated at my son's school about a sex offender. Megan's Law requires that the community must be informed of the name and address of a convicted sex offender in the neighborhood. I was comforted in knowing that my son knows to inform me if he is violated in any way, by anyone, family or stranger. He knows I will listen and believe him.

"The 'Tell Mommy and Daddy Everything--No Secrets Rule' is very powerful information to give to a child. It was very empowering for me as a parent to know that I can protect my child from the childhood I had. I believe that my children are growing up with a strong belief that their body is theirs. Dorothy's book has been my main guide in teaching my child self-protection. I use these principles and concepts to measure other parenting books. I highly recommend this book to every parent, grandparent, and anyone who has child care responsibility.

"Thank you, Dorothy, for speaking the truth about this crime being committed by family members that heretofore was not spoken about."

Chapter One

A Mother's Story--Sexual Abuse and Incest are Perpetrated Anywhere, Anytime, and by Someone You Least Expect

The following is a dialog and thought process derived from a mother's true story:

"Mommy, can I take my panties off outside?" my 3½-year-old daughter, Cindy, asked as we walked across the street to our house; this followed her visit with her friend Gretchen.

My mind raced to what could have possibly prompted her to ask such a question. In spite of my fear, I calmly asked, "What were you playing?"

"Hide-and-seek, and Billy (Gretchen's brother, 13) was in the tree fort."

"Did your panties get wet?"

"No, Billy said, 'Take your panties off.'"

"Did you?"

"Gretchen took hers off."

"Did you take yours off?"

"No, Gretchen said it was OK."

When we got inside, I asked her to show me what Gretchen did, to make sure I understood. With that she pulled her panties down and "mooned" the air with a bare bottom. I did not expect this demonstration. This disturbed me.

"Did he touch you?"

"No," she responded.

Although he had not touched her, Billy had violated her and his sister. I would not have suspected this behavior, not from this family. These parents were pillars of the community and trusted neighbors, a college dean and a preschool administrator. My thoughts were racing--"How could this happen, their mother was home supervising the children playing?"

My mind darted back to a few weeks earlier, when Billy had stayed with my daughter while I ran errands. After questioning her, I was confident no violation occurred then. However, this "mooning" game, readily demonstrated by his sister, was an indication Gretchen had done it before and now she had encouraged and coached her playmate (my daughter) to do the same.

Feeling obligated to other children who played with Gretchen, I reported the incident to Child Protective Services and learned the violation with

Gretchen went beyond "mooning" Billy as he requested.

According to the current definition of sexual abuse and incest from E. Sue Blume's book, *Secret Survivors*, Billy was sexually violating both girls: "If it [the experience] is unwanted or inappropriate for her age or the relationship, it is abuse. If she is forced to see what she does not want to see that is abuse."

Unfortunately, Cindy's experience is more common than we could ever imagine. Further, the compulsion to act out sexual urges does not go away by itself. Therefore, without intervention, Billy would repeat this incident or he would escalate to more blatant sexual activity. Fortunately for Cindy, she could protect herself because she understood the "your body is yours" concept, which prompted her to question her conflict. Although Gretchen complied, through Cindy's belief that "the sanctity and control of your body are yours," she was able to resist and then clarify her experience. She was one of the lucky ones; her mother had taught, demonstrated and enforced concepts of self-protection.

To protect your child from sexual abuse you need to know:

1. What sexual abuse or incest is;
2. What to do;
3. How to teach your child self-protection.

Chapter Two

Sexual Abuse and Incest--An Overview

Sexual abuse and incest have come out of the closet thanks to many brave women and men who went public with society's most guarded, taboo subjects. These people were abused by someone they knew--family members, family friends, neighbors, teachers, clergy and child caretakers. In spite of increased publicity, tragically we still want to cling to the belief that strangers sexually abuse most of our children--the "scruffy old man" in disheveled clothes and day-old beard. We also want to believe sexual abuse or incest by family members is something that happens only to "other people," the ones on the "other side of town" who do not have a good education, jobs or affluence.

The first response we form when hearing of sexual abuse or incest is denial: "I do not have to be concerned about that in my community. This would never happen in my family."

The unbelievable reality is that a person who sexually abuses children may seem very average and ordinary to the world. He or she may be a leader in the church, in the community or in business. He or she does not fit a classic stereotype and is not necessarily uneducated, unemployed, impoverished or an alcoholic.

We find sexual abuse and incest even more difficult to believe or accept when the person we like, admire, love, and/or marry is the perpetrator of the abuse. Tragically, the unwillingness to accept the facts concerning sexual abuse perpetrators leaves children vulnerable to becoming victims and increases the likelihood that they will be abused.

Common Myths about Child Sexual Abuse and Incest

Myth: Children lie or fantasize about sexual activities with adults.

Fact: Using developmental terms, young children cannot make up explicit sexual information. They must be exposed to it to speak about it. Sometimes a parent will coach a child to report sexual abuse falsely. The key indicators of the falseness in such a report are the child's inability to describe explicit details, the inability to illustrate the act, or gross inconsistencies within the account.

Myth: Most victims of sexual abuse are teenaged girls.

Fact: While more girls than boys are sexually abused, many are abused before their first birthday.

Myth: Boys can't be sexually abused.
Fact: Masculine gender socialization instills in boys the belief they are to be strong; they should learn to protect themselves. In truth, boys are children and are as vulnerable as girls. They cannot really fight back against the perpetrator. A perpetrator generally has greater size, strength, knowledge, or a position of authority, using such resources as money or other bribes, or outright threats--whatever advantage the perpetrator can take to get what they want.

Myth: Sexual abuse of a child is usually an isolated, one-time incident.
Fact: Child sexual abuse and incest occurrences develop gradually, over time; often, repeat occurrences are generally the rule rather than the exception.

Myth: Children will naturally outgrow the effects of sexual abuse or incest.
Fact: Sexual abuse or incest affects every aspect of human development. The damage is profound, extensive and pervasive. It is deeper than the physical and emotional level--it is a soul injury that requires multifaceted, multidimensional, therapeutic processing conducted by a psychotherapist who specializes in sexual abuse and incest trauma recovery.

Myth: Non-violent sexual behavior between a child and an adult is not emotionally damaging to the child.
Fact: Although child sexual abuse often involves subtle rather than extreme force, nearly all survivors experience confusion, shame, guilt, anger, as well as a lowered sense of self-esteem; these are classic aftereffects, although they may not initially reveal obvious signs.

Myth: Child molesters are all "dirty old men."
Fact: In a recent study of convicted child molesters, 80 percent committed their first offense before age 30.

Myth: Children provoke sexual abuse by their seductive behavior.
Fact: Seductive behavior may be the result, but is never the cause of sexual abuse. Amy Fisher, the Long Island teenager who shot her perpetrator's wife in the face and whom the media dubbed, "Lolita," is a perfect example of this myth. During her trial for attempting to kill Joey Buttafuoco's wife, Amy Fisher revealed that she had been sexually abused before her abuse by Buttafuoco. Her behavior that many considered seductive and promiscuous may have, in fact, been a result of prior abuse. However, regardless of the victim's behavior or reason for such behavior, the responsibility for appropriate behavior always lies with the adult, not the child.

Myth: If children wanted to avoid sexual advances of adults, or persons in positions of greater power, they could say, "Stop" or "No."

Fact: Children generally do not question the behavior of adults. In addition, bribes, threats, flattery, trickery and use of authority coerce them.

Myth: When a child is sexually abused, it is immediately apparent.

Fact: In cases of incest against children, as much as the perpetrator might be hurting the victim, the child loves him or her and needs her family. Therefore, she convinces herself that she is somehow causing him or her to behave this way, and she remains silent. In her confusion of loyalty to her perpetrator, she protects him or her by holding the secret. Thus, she carries the shame and guilt. In cases regarding sexual abuse and incest, the victim often believes that she has "cooperated" with the perpetrator in some way and places inappropriate blame on herself. Therefore, although with tremendous suffering, she hides her pain through denial, dissociation, numbing, zoning out, hyperactivity, as well as other distracting behaviors. However, the aware parent would recognize these behaviors as a sign that "something is wrong." These behaviors and signs of sexual abuse of children will be further discussed and detailed in Chapter 6.

Myth: When the sexual abuse victim is male, male homosexuals are the abuse perpetrators.

Fact: Most child sexual abuse is perpetrated by heterosexual men, who do not find sex with other men satisfactory. Many child molesters, even though they are heterosexual, abuse both boys and girls.

Myth: Boys abused by males are or will become homosexual.

Fact: Whether victimized by males or females, boys' or girls' premature sexual experiences are damaging in many ways, including confusion about their sexual identity and orientation.

Myth: When a boy and a woman take part in sexual behavior and it is the boy's idea, he is not being abused.

Fact: Child abuse is an act of power by which an adult uses a child. Abuse is abuse; a woman engaging in sexual behavior with a male child is still sexually abusive, even if she thinks he initiated the contact.

Myth: If the perpetrator is female, the boy or adolescent is fortunate to have been initiated into heterosexual activity.

Fact: Premature or coerced sex, whether by a mother, aunt, sister, babysitter or other female causes confusion, at best, and rage, depression or other problems in more negative circumstances. Whether male or female, to be used as a sexual object is always abusive and damaging.

Myth: If the child experiences sexual arousal or orgasm from abuse, he or she has been a willing participant or enjoyed it.

Fact: Children can respond physically to stimulation (get an erection) even in traumatic or painful sexual situations. A perpetrator can maintain secrecy by labeling the child's sexual response as an indication of his or her willingness to participate. "You liked it, you wanted it." The survivor is then manipulated with their own guilt and shame because they experienced physical arousal while being abused. Physical, visual or auditory stimulation is likely to occur in a sexual situation. It does not mean the child wanted the experience or understood what it meant.

Myth: Males who were sexually abused as boys all grow up to sexually abuse children.
Fact: Only some sexually abused boys become perpetrators of sexual abuse.

Myth: Boys are less traumatized as victims of sexual abuse than girls.
Fact: Studies show that long-term effects are equally damaging for either sex. Ironically, males may be more damaged by society's refusal or reluctance to accept their victimization, and by their resultant belief that they must "tough it out" in silence.

Myth: If a child is sexually active with his or her peers, then it is not sexual abuse.
Fact: The act is abusive if the child is induced into sexual activity with anyone who is in a position of greater power, whether that power is derived through the perpetrator's age, size, status, or relationship. A child who cannot refuse, or who believes she or he cannot refuse, is a child who has been violated.

History of and Facts Regarding Sexual Abuse and Incest

Extensive evidence substantiates the fact that sexual abuse of children has taken place for centuries. D. Corwin (1990) cites that in London many believed that sexual "congress" with a child would cure venereal disease. Of capital rape prosecutions between 1730 and 1790, 25 percent of the cases involved victims younger than 10 years old. Other documented evidence includes:

   -*1858-1869* in France--three quarters of those charged with rape during this time period were accused of raping children.

   -*1874* in New York--the first American Society for the Prevention of Cruelty to Children was founded.

   -*1896* in *The Aetiology of Hysteria*, Freud discusses his "Seduction Theory" acknowledging the sexual abuse and incest of children.

   -*Late 19th Century*--British and American feminists, church members and sex reformers argue that incest occurs in all social classes.

While prohibitions have existed opposing the sexual abuse and/or incest of children since ancient times, and both primitive as well as modern cultures have provided strong penalties for breaking these prohibitions, including death, the incidents of sexual abuse or incest continue to increase dramatically.

Unfortunately, accurate statistics regarding sexual abuse and/or incest are difficult to obtain because different definitions of sexual abuse and incest will result in different statistics. Self-reporting is only accurate if the victim accepts the same definition of sexual abuse or incest as defined by the researcher. Even more frustrating is the fact that many survivors do not remember their abuse. However, this does not mean they do not suffer aftereffects of the abuse. To the contrary, although these women have not remembered their abuse, they suffer tremendously not knowing why.

The controversy regarding the phenomenon of whether a person can "forget" something as significant as sexual activity has been thoroughly studied. The Betrayal trauma theory has most accurately identified the child's experience. "[The] Betrayal trauma theory suggests that psychogenic amnesia is an adaptive response to childhood abuse. When a parent or other powerful figure violates a fundamental ethic of human relationships, victims may need to remain unaware of the trauma not to reduce suffering but rather to promote survival. Amnesia enables the child to maintain an attachment with a figure vital to survival, development, and thriving" (E. Sue Blume, *Secret Survivors*).

There are several independent surveys and studies regarding the prevalence of sexual abuse and incest survivors who do not remember their abuse for varied periods of time. In a clinical sample of incest survivors conducted by J. Herman and E. Schatzow in the late 1980s, 28 percent reported severe memory deficits. Sixty-four percent reported some degree of amnesia. In a 1994 national sample of psychologists, conducted by S. Feldman-Summers and K. Pope, 23.9 percent reported childhood abuse. Of the psychologists who recounted abuse, 40 percent reported some period of time when victims forgot some or all of the abuse.

In a prospective study of women's memories of child sexual abuse conducted by L. Williams in 1994, 38 percent of the women studied did not recall sexual abuse that had been reported and documented in a hospital emergency room 17 years earlier. Women who were younger at the time of the abuse were more likely to have no recall of the abuse. In a survey conducted by E. Loftus, S. Polonsky and M. Fullilove in 1994, 54 percent of the 105 women in an out-patient treatment for substance abuse reported themselves as victims of past sexual abuse; nineteen percent reported they forgot the abuse over time, but the memory returned later. In 1993, J. Briere and J. Conte conducted a self-report survey for abuse in adults molested as children. This self-report survey revealed 59 percent of 450 women and men in treatment for sexual abuse at some time before age 18 had forgotten the sexual abuse.

Another reason statistics are difficult to obtain is because many children die before they are identified as having been sexually abused. JonBenèt Ramsey, the 6 year-old beauty pageant contestant from Boulder, Colorado, has been identified by several professionals, including myself, as a classic victim of sexual abuse. JonBenèt displayed several signs of child sexual abuse. The most obvious sign was her sexy behavior in routines at pageants, as seen on television.

It is shocking and horrifying that those people around her did not recognize or question the signs of sexual abuse, including her pediatrician, Dr. Francesco Beuf. Dr. Beuf has confirmed that he gave JonBenèt six vaginal examinations during 27 visits in a three-year period because of symptoms of painful urination and genital redness (Sawyer, September 1997 and Krupski, *The Boulder Daily Camera*, February 1997). Although Dr. Beuf states he considers the complaints and frequency not unusual in little girls, other professionals disagree. Dr. David Soper, professor of gynecology at the University of South Carolina said: "This is certainly not consistent with my experience. It's highly unlikely that a child of 6 would have recurring vaginitis." Furthermore, Dr. Wendy Maltz, author of *Incest and Sexuality: A Guide to Understanding and Healing*, says that painful urination along with vaginal itching and redness are definitely signs of sexual abuse. As stated in the article "Missing Innocence," by Ann Bardach, "Vaginitis six times in three years is NOT normal" (*Vanity Fair*, October 29, 1997).

The fact she had 27 visits in a three-year period indicates something unusual is going on. Children who are healthy mentally and physically do not go to a doctor 27 times in three years. Having heard countless stories from survivors, I concur with Drs. Soper and Maltz.

Her parents have confirmed while interviewed that JonBenèt frequently wet the bed, which is another classic sign of sexual abuse. This fact has been dismissed by the Ramseys as nothing unusual for a 6-year old. JonBenèt's father, John Ramsey, in an interview with Katie Couric, NBC *Today Show* March 20-24, 2000, confirmed the frequent doctor visits, stating that they had good insurance coverage and the doctor's office was near their home.

One has to question this logic. How many 6-year-olds who frequently wet the bed do you know? How many parents take their child to the doctor because they have good insurance and the doctor's office is nearby? It is curious to note that when given the opportunity to refute inflammatory information, the Ramseys have not always done so.

When both the bedwetting and vaginal problems are considered, JonBenèt's pediatrician had an obligation to report the facts to Child Protective Services, which is charged with the responsibility of investigating these types of reports to determine if the facts are conclusive of sexual abuse and taking appropriate action. Having heard countless stories similar to this from sexual abuse survivors, the signs are unmistakable.

As further indication of JonBenèt's victimization, Dr. Robert Kirshner, former medical examiner in the Chicago University pathology department, reported that JonBenèt's autopsy showed that the opening in her vagina was twice as wide as a normal 6-year-old's. This is an indication of penetration, which would be apparent to any doctor (Bardach, "Missing Innocence," *Vanity Fair*, October 29, 1997).

Furthermore, Dr. Cyril Wecht, a noted coroner from Allegheny County, Pa., former president of the American Academy of Forensic Science and co-author of the book, *Who Killed JonBenèt Ramsey?* stated that he was convinced she was abused regularly. "There is absolutely no question she was abused. There's blood and contusions [in the vagina and the hymen has been torn]." He further stated, "If she'd gone to a big city hospital and a doctor had examined her genitals, any adult male in her home would have been arrested" (Maloney, *Crime Magazine*, December 1998, and Krupski, *The Boulder Daily Camera*, Feb 15, 1997).

ABC—September 13, 1999, *Good Morning America's* Elizabeth Vargas interviewed Linda Arndt, former Boulder, Colorado police detective, who was present at the time John Ramsey found JonBenèt stated, "The trauma was consistent with injuries seen in sexual assault cases."

In addition to the above signs, *Globe* (August 1997) included these additional signs of sexual abuse.

-Isolation or withdrawal: Pageant professionals reportedly noticed JonBenèt was robot-like. "She was like a machine. She would sit quiet and unemotional until she had to perform." Abused children often feel alone and helpless and withdraw into a shell.

-Difficulty walking: Photographers reportedly stated that JonBenèt was sometimes unsteady on her feet. If a child is unsteady on his or her feet—one needs to wonder what is causing the unsteadiness. The unsteadiness could be caused by emotional and physical pain or body damage; such as (in the case of a girl) dislocated back, hips or pelvis.

-Fear of the bathroom: Reportedly several adults in the pageant community said there was a constant battle between JonBenèt and her mother regarding using the bathroom. Was it a battle of wills or avoiding urinating because urinating was painful? One has to wonder what this was about. If it was caused by painful urination what was the cause? Coupled with other sexual abuse signs this behavior would raise questions and applying the "Appropriate Suspicion" rule and trusting your "Intuition" is warranted (discussed in Chapter 5).

-Violent behavior: Reportedly, one photographer remembers seeing JonBenèt kick her mother. Sexual abuse survivors feel extreme frustration, anger and sometimes lash out.

Other publications also reported evidence of long-term sexual abuse.

B. J. Plasket, reporter for Longmont FYI—*Daily Times*—Call, July 15, 1997, "Autopsy Raises More Questions," quotes Dr. Wecht, Allegheny County, Pa. coroner and pathologist in a CNBC news interview, "This was a part of a sexual game that had been played before. I don't see how anyone can say there was not a sexual assault."

Pam Regensberg, reporter for Longmont FYI—Daily Times—Call, August 13, 1997, "Pathologist: JonBenèt Murder Unintentional" quoted Dr. Wecht, "It was a sex game gone bad. This was not an intentional killing. Nobody was out to kill the girl." Dr. Wecht stated further, "The case bears resemblance to those in which auto-asphyxiation or oxygen deprivation during a sex act is involved."

The most thorough and compelling analysis of JonBenèt's death and suspected sexual abuse was made by Andrew G. Hodges, M.D., in his book, *A Mother Gone*

Bad—the hidden confession of JonBenèt's killer. Hodges analyzed the ransom note word for word, including, writing style using a technique called, "psycholinguistics." He posits the ransom note reveals Patsy Ramsey killed JonBenèt and furthermore, she knew for some period of time that John Ramsey was sexually abusing JonBenèt.

Hodges sites the following two statements in the ransom note to be the strongest unintentional confession to the sexual abuse of JonBenèt by John Ramsey.

"Make sure that you bring an adequate size attache to the bank." "If we monitor you getting the money early, we might call you early to arrange an earlier delivery of the money and hence, a [sic] earlier (delivery—word crossed out) pick-up of your daughter." Hodges contends, "The message suggests that prior to the murder Patsy unexpectedly came across her husband molesting JonBenèt—taking her valuables from her, intruding into JonBenèt's 'bank.' 'Bank' is the symbolic meaning for a woman, and the woman being talked about is JonBenèt. Using the instruction 'bring an adequate size attachè,' tells the reader not to miss the connection between the attachè and a small container like a small little girl. Another meaning for 'early' is 'young'—JonBenèt's valuables were removed before she was of age. Patsy is telling us that after discovering her husband's sexual gratification/abuse, she unexpectedly then had to communicate with him—call him—and this caused the situation to escalate. Patsy further reveals that deep down she had known that some sort of explosion leading to JonBenèt's death was going to take place, and that it still had consciously occurred unexpectedly—earlier." Since 'pick-up' is slang for sexual promiscuity, Hodges contends Patsy is confessing that JonBenèt is the one being 'picked-up' by John, something sexual was going on between them. 'Pick-up' could also refer to Patsy and John's ongoing sexual exploitation of JonBenèt through pageants.

FBI special agent, Charles Donald Byron, wrote an endorsement for Hodges' book stating, "As a seasoned, skeptical FBI agent---I am now convinced that his [Hodges'] in-depth analysis of the ransom communication tells us who the killer is...."

James O. Raney, M.D., Clinical Associate Professor in Psychiatry, University of Washington School of Medicine, Seattle, wrote an endorsement, stating, "This is a story of jealousy, envy, terror, revenge, love and hate. The participants try to cover an event that is the stuff of classic drama, and of our own unthinkable unconscious minds. Provocative, original, richly detailed, and hard to refute, Dr. Hodges' argument is compelling." Whether we believe Dr. Hodges' analysis or other professional's opinions, the "Appropriate Suspicion" rule and using one's intuition needs to be applied. (discussed in Chapter 5.)

CU Medical School Dean Dr. Richard Krugman, who served as a consultant to the investigation, is among those not convinced of sexual abuse. He said, "I don't see anything that tells me with certainty that she was sexually assaulted. I look at this and see a child who was physically abused and is dead. I don't think it's possible to tell whether any child was sexually abused based on physical findings alone."

Professional denial or trivilization is not some modern phenomenon concocted in the last decade of the 20th century but, rather, a secret with a long history. Dr. Sigmund Freud was the first to come face to face with universal professional denial when he abandoned his seduction theory (his belief that most of the psychological problems his upper-class female patients had were due to sexual abuse by their fathers). His work was vigorously refuted. Due to professional pressures, he subsequently adopted the theory of the Oedipal and Oedipus complex as an explanation for his patients' problems and continued working with them in a futile effort to relieve their suffering. This theory did not, however, resolve the tremendous suffering women and men endured.

Whatever the obstacles have been, many courageous researchers continue to report their findings, thereby giving society the opportunity to decide whether to ignore the findings or do something to foster change. One researcher, Diana Russell who has gained highly-regarded recognition as a family violence researcher, states:

"Incestuous [sexual] abuse can no longer be viewed as a problem that involves a few sick or disturbed sex offenders. Particularly when considered along with spouse rape, wife-beating and non-sexual child abuse, it reveals an intensely troubled contemporary family. The fact that the vast majority of this abuse is being perpetrated by males suggests that a full understanding of this problem requires seeing it within the context of severe gender and generation inequality."

David Finkelhor and Russell have been credited for the most comprehensive study on sexual abuse and incest. According to Finkelhor, estimates of female sexual abuse survivors range from 6 percent to 62 percent, while estimates for males vary from 3 percent to 31 percent. Russell's study revealed 38 percent of women survivors were abused before age 18. Furthermore, Finkelhor and J. Dziuba-Leatherman, in a 1992 national survey asking adult women about their lifetime experiences of rape, reported there is a five-fold higher rape risk for children--61 percent of rapes occur before age 18.

Other statistics include:

– The typical child sex offender molests an average of 117 children, most do not report the offense - National Institute of Mental Health, 1988.

– About 60 percent of male survivors sampled reported at least one of their perpetrators to be female - Mendel, 1993.

– About 95 percent of victims know their perpetrators - CCPCA, 1992.

– It is estimated that approximately 71percent of child sex offenders are under 35 and knew the victim at least casually. About 80 percent of these individuals are within normal intelligence ranges; 59 percent gain sexual access to their victims through seduction or enticement - Burgess & Groth, 1980.

- The U.S. Department of Justice reported 4 million child sexual abuse and incest perpetrators reside in the United States - *Network News*, Fall Edition, 1986.

- Nearly half of all sex offenders are less than 18 years old - FBI Uniform Crime Report, 1991.

- There are 755 juvenile sex offender rehabilitation programs. In 1983 there were 22 programs - Holmes, January 18, 1993.

- A total of 10,000 female children under age 18 were raped in 1992, 3,800 girls were under 12. Twenty percent were raped by their fathers, 26 percent by other relatives, and 50 percent by friends and associates. Only 4 percent were raped by strangers - The U.S. Justice Department, study conducted in 11 states and the District of Columbia, June 1994.

- Thirty men were charged with more than 1,300 counts of sexual crimes against 50 boys. The pedophiles included social workers, schoolteachers and politicians. Victims were as young as 8 years old. Police confiscated more than 1,200 homemade videos and hundreds of Polaroid photos and child-porn magazines - Reuters News Agency, June 1994.

- Rape arrests of 13-year-old males in New York City increased 200 percent between 1986 and 1988 - Gore, January 1990.

- "The sexual exploitation of children is the basis for the production and distribution of child pornography." - Attorney General's Commission on Pornography, 1986.

- Of child sexual abuse and incest perpetrators, 57 percent are survivors of sexual abuse that occurred in their childhood - Goldstein-Harte Study 1973: Carter, et al, "Use of Pornography in the Criminal and Developmental Histories of Sexual Offenders," 1984.

- Sixty percent of adult prostitutes have been sexually abused by an average of two males each, some by as many as eleven different males; 90 percent knew their abusers. Sixty percent of prostitutes in this study were 16 or under. Many were younger than 13 and almost 80 percent had become prostitutes before age 18 – Silber and Pines, "Effects of Child Sexual Abuse" study.

- Ninety-two percent of teenage prostitutes were sexually molested in childhood - Janus, 1981.

- Perpetrators abuse between 30 and 60 children before they are arrested--as many as 380 during their lifetime - "The Effects of Pornography on Children and Women," Hearings before the Subcommittee of Juvenile Justice, Committee on the Judiciary U.S. Senate (testimony of John Rabun, for the National Center for Missing and Exploited Children, September 1984).

- Rates of assault, rape and robbery against children 12 to 19 years old are two to three times higher than for the adult population - according to a National Crime Survey, 1990.

– Edward Donnerstein compared the effects of erotica (sexual consent without violence) and pornography (sexual activity that was violent and abusive). Male college students (prescreened to eliminate abnormally hostile individuals) were exposed to erotica and pornography; their erotic response was much higher to pornography.

– Ninety-six percent of female rape victims younger than 12 years old knew their attackers - U.S. Department of Justice, 1992.

– There are more than 58 million adult survivors of incest and child sexual abuse in America. Over 85 percent of the perpetrators were adults the child knew and trusted. Over 80 percent of the mothers of incest victims were also victimized as children. Of teenage, unwed mothers, 60 to 67 percent were incest victims. Over 50 percent of the children whose parents are in custody and court cases in the family and dependency courts are returned to the sole custody of the parent accused of abuse – *Los Angeles Times* survey, 1993.

Statistics notwithstanding, sexual abuse and incest against female victims is so common it can be considered an epidemic. Many women come to therapy with various physical and emotional complaints. Many, if not most, survivors do not attribute the cause of their problems to sexual abuse or incest trauma. They attribute their complaints to their inadequacy in handling the rigors of adult life. These complaints include, but are not limited to: gastrointestinal disorders, gynecological disorders, headaches, arthritis, joint pain, eating disorders, alcohol or drug abuse, phobias, depression, low self-esteem, suicidal thoughts or attempts, nightmares of threat or entrapment, inability to trust or trusting indiscriminately. These complaints are so indicative of sexual abuse that E. Sue Blume, author of *Secret Survivors* compiled a checklist of 34 major characteristics (aftereffects).

Because of a child's innocence and often dependence on the abuser, sexual abuse is not only a violation of her body and boundaries, it is a violation of her trust. In this respect, the sexual aspect is secondary. The person she trusted with her innocence, instead of giving her love, has taken what he wanted from her, terrorized her, hurt her, humiliated her, controlled her, disgraced her, and shattered her perception of herself and her relationship with him. Although he emphasized his love for her, he perpetrated a violence that did not require force. In this violence, described as love, he robbed her of the opportunity to develop into a healthy, adjusted adult. He abrogated his responsibility to care for and protect her.

This insidious betrayal so profoundly affects a child's sense of trust that she works mightily to regain fully what should have been a birthright. Whether the assault occurred once or several times is irrelevant, since the damage is incurred immediately. This damage is profound, extensive and pervasive. Sexual abuse and incest affect every aspect of human development. A soul injury forms as the result of sexual abuse; an injury that time, education, job, money, marriage, children, moving, or divorce cannot heal. An injury so deeply wounding and traumatizing that it requires more for resolution than reading books, self-help groups or undertaking intellectual analysis. Children or adults who have been victims do not "get over" the devastation of sexual abuse or incest as they would with the measles or a virus. Millions of adult survivors continue to bear the emotional scars of childhood sexual abuse or incest.

As one survivor told me, she believed that her abuse was minor in nature and that she could, "put it behind me." At the age of 42, she decided to engage in therapy because she had developed a psychosomatic skin condition. "I had used the stiff-upper-lip method, not realizing all the pain I had was directly related to the sexual abuse," she confided, adding, "I wish I had gone to therapy years ago." When she heard I was writing this book she said, "Be sure to tell survivors to go for therapy and remain in therapy until they are completely healed."

"When childhood sexual abuse is not treated, society must later deal with the resulting problems, including crime, suicide, alcohol or drug use, and more sexual abuse," stated Dr. William C. Holmes of the University of Pennsylvania School of Medicine. His studies revealed that one-third of juvenile delinquents, 40 percent of sexual offenders and 76 percent of serial rapists report they were sexually abused as youngsters. The suicide rate among sexually abused boys was as significant as 14 times higher than that among non-victims; reports of multiple substance abuse among sixth-grade boys who were molested were 12 to 40 times greater than compared to non-victims.

In my practice, I have listened to countless stories of sexual abuse. I think I have heard it all, only to hear another survivor's story of abuse so horrendous; I have tears of compassion.

Who is the Perpetrator?

The existence of sexual feelings toward family members does not signify a problem. However, the acts of focusing on and then reinforcing these feelings creates a compulsion to carry out acts of sexual abuse and negates one's sense of discipline and self-control, thus forming an arousal pattern. To act on this arousal pattern and the impulses he or she has created, the abuser insidiously justifies his or her behavior to himself or herself.

The perpetrator rationalizes and/or minimizes his or her actions as well as the consequences to himself or herself and his or her victims. Perpetrators convince themselves that the child won't remember, or they justify to themselves denial of responsibility to the child if the child does remember the abuse. They protect themselves by manipulating the child into being a co-conspirator or forcing the child to take responsibility either through intimidation, threats or sometimes even physical violence. They tell the child such things as:

- "It is our 'secret.'"
- "I am doing this because I love you."
- "I think you are special. Don't you want to be Daddy's girl?"
- "You are prettier than Mommy."
- "You enjoy it as much as I do."

- "It won't hurt."
- "You are a liar/whore anyway and asked for it."
- "You took the money."
- "I am only teaching you the realities of life."
- "Your mother does not show me any affection."

Other forms of justification/manipulation practiced by the perpetrator include:

- In cases where the mother is the perpetrator, the act is often in the guise of caring for the child.
- In some instances when the mother is a perpetrator it has been at the instigation and encouragement of the father, her husband.

One woman told me that when she confronted her father for raping her at age 17, he calmly replied, "I have asked for God's forgiveness and you should too." She was shocked at his matter-of-fact negation for what he had done and his implication he believed she was equally responsible.

Perpetrators often justify their actions by aggrandizing their authority: "I am a good [father, grandfather, uncle, a good provider.] I am your [father, grandfather, mother], I can do what I want. I put food on the table and clothes on your back. You are too sexy and pretty. I cannot control myself." He silences her with consequences if she tells:

- "I could go to jail."
- "You will break up the family."
- "Do you want the police to come?"
- "Mommy will hate you for making Daddy go away."

- "The family will have no money and no food; everyone will be sad, and it will be your fault."
- "Nobody will believe you."

After awhile the perpetrator believes his or her own lies. The abuser becomes an expert at manipulation; they escape adult reality, and are good at pretending that their behavior is not harming the child. They may expend great energy maintaining this illusion to themselves as well as others. They create a persona of goodness beyond reproach. Anyone who sees through this façade is met with admonishment and rebuke for being critical, irrational and/or jealous. The perpetrator is the family *emperor with no clothes.*

Sexual abusing behavior is seldom the case of only one family member gone amuck. Many perpetrators are victims themselves, who have passed through the generations from victimizer to a victim-become victimizer or to victim become mother-of-victim.

Russell reports that 60 percent of child sexual abuse offenders are relatives of their victims and 29 percent are acquaintances. While only 11 percent are the classic stereotypes, "the stranger lurking near the playground," we still cling to the belief that our children are most at peril with strangers who sexually abuse.

There is no single cause for sexual abuse. Indeed, it is a complex issue. K. Meiselman classified and described incestuous fathers in seven categories.

1. Endogamic (68 percent). These men are described as heavily dependent (codependent) on their families for emotional and sexual needs; they are unwilling or unable

to satisfy sexual needs appropriately. This group was broken down into the following two subgroups: personality disorder and sub-cultural variety. The men who were described as having a personality disorder were often shy and ineffectual in social relationships. They often think with some degree of paranoia and are over-controlling, preoccupied with sex and often sexually involved with a prepubescent daughter. The men in the sub-cultural group were from isolated rural areas that were semi-tolerant of incest and were moralistic.

2. Psychopathic (10 percent). These men frequently have criminal records and are generally sexually promiscuous, with little emotional attachment to their victims. Psychopathic is used infrequently to define a perpetrator profile. It usually refers to a person with a personality disorder that causes them to behave in socially unacceptable ways, without having regrets or feeling guilt.

3. Psychotic (5 percent). These men have been described as having a lack of appropriate ego boundaries. People diagnosed as having a psychotic disorder commonly have trouble with reality testing, have delusions, hallucinations, and inappropriate mood reactions.

4. Drunken (5 percent). The incest took place when the father was "extremely intoxicated." Often, drunken perpetrators do not remember the abuse due to an alcohol blackout.

5. Pedophilic (11 percent). Usually these men are attracted to young children as sex partners and subsequently lose sexual interest when the child develops secondary sex characteristics. The American Psychiatric Association defines pedophilia as a sexual disorder, with the essential characteristic described as: "recurrent intense sexual urges and sexually arousing fantasies involving sexual activity with a prepubescent child (frequently 13 years old or younger)."

6. Mentally Defective (less than 1 percent). This group of men is of such low intelligence that there is a reduced ability to manage ego controls.

7. Situational (less than 1 percent). This category was developed for incest that occurred only during times of high stress for the perpetrator.

Frequently, perpetrators are sexual or physical abuse survivors themselves and they are acting out their pain. Although Meiselman does not include this type of category or sub-category, I have treated perpetrators whose actions were clearly and irrefutably linked to their past experiences of physical and/or sexual abuse.

Women, having the major and constant involvement as mothers with the intimate physical functions of rearing and caring for children, are less likely to abuse than are men. Both Diana Russell and David Finkelhor, family violence researchers, estimate women perpetrators account for only 20 percent when both male and female survivors are considered.

The acceptance that women are perpetrators is more complicated and more controversial than the acceptance that male perpetrators exist. Ironically, then, characteristics of female sexual abuse perpetrators have been researched and studied extensively by numerous researchers. Although some researchers differ on the characteristics of female perpetrators, their conclusions that females are less likely to sexually abuse boys or girls is unanimous.

A study by researchers Matthew, Matthews, and Speltz (1989) and Patton (1987) of female sexual offenders who were in the Genesis II treatment project in Minnesota, revealed all but one of the women were themselves victims of childhood sexual abuse and many were also victims of physical abuse. There are compelling and consistent patterns of childhood social isolation, alienation, and lack of development of interpersonal skills and competence among these women perpetrators. Three categories of female sex offenders emerged and were further described as: Teacher/Lover, Predisposed (intergenerational), and Male-Coerced.

- *The Teacher/Lover* engages prepubescent and adolescent males with whom she relates to as a peer. Her motive is, ostensibly, to teach her young victims about sexuality.

- *The Predisposed* offender is frequently a victim of severe sexual abuse that was initiated at a very young age and persisted over a long period of time. She initiates the sexual abuse and the victims are usually her own children. Her motives are non-threatening emotional intimacy.

- *The Male-Coerced* offender engages initially in conjunction with a male who has previously abused children, which could include her children. She acts out a pattern of extreme dependency and nonassertive behavior, and she may initiate sexual abuse herself. Her victims are children both within and outside of the family.

Faller (1987) reported on 40 women who were judged by clinical staff to have sexually abused at least 63 children. These women represented 14 percent of the total 289 perpetrators of sexual abuse. Many of the women had significant difficulties in psychological and social functioning. About half of the women had mental problems, both retardation and psychotic illness. More than half had chemical dependency problems, and close to three-fourths had maltreated their victims in other ways in addition to the sexual abuse. The women were categorized into the five case types that follow (four were sexually abusive in more than one context).

1. *Polyincestuous abuse.* Twenty-nine (72.5 percent) of the women studied belong in this category. In this type of abuse, there are a minimum of two perpetrators and generally two or more victims. Usually, a male rather than the female offender instigated the abuse. The woman went along with the male and played a secondary role.

2. *Single-parent abuse.* Six (15 percent) of the women studied were single parents. These mothers did not have ongoing relationships with men and the oldest child seemed to serve as a surrogate partner for the mother, often having adult role responsibilities.

3. *Psychotic abuser.* Only three (7.5 percent) of the women were classified as psychotic at the time of perpetrating the sexual abuse. Therefore, this study did not support the clinical assumption that most female perpetrators are highly disturbed and often psychotic at the time of the sexual abuse.

4. *Adolescent perpetrators.* Three (7.5 percent) were adolescent girls who had difficulty with peer relationships and lacked alternative sexual outlets.

5. *Non-custodial abusers.* There was only one woman who was the non- custodial mother of her victims and sexually abused the children during visitation. Faller believes that in such cases the non-custodial parent is apt to be devastated at the loss of her spouse and the children then become the source of emotional gratification.

Faller concludes that the circumstances that lead women to sexually abuse children can be differentiated from those causing men to do so.

McCarthy (1986) describes the profile of 26 offenders of mother-child incest. These women were studied by the Dallas Incest Treatment Program over a three-year period and constituted 4 percent of the offender population. The incidents had been validated by a protective service investigation. Nine of the mothers were co-offenders with a male partner, while the remaining were independent offenders (a male offender was also involved in half of these). All but two of the women described their childhood as difficult and abusive. When the mother was a co-offender, her dependency on her spouse was the major contributing factor. Three cases were mother-son incest— the father was out of the home and the mothers seemed to treat the boys as age-equal mates. The women who abused their daughters seemed to treat the daughters as extensions of themselves. Half of these women were of borderline intelligence. It is significant to note the independent offenders were characterized as experiencing themselves psychologically as loners and lacking any sense of attachment or belonging. They were likely to have married as teenagers. Half of the offenders were characterized as seriously emotionally disturbed and almost half had a serious chemical abuse problem. It is also noteworthy all of the independent offenders were reportedly of average intelligence.

Vander Mey (1988) reviews the research on sexually abused boys and reports that there is so little information on sexual abuse of males that findings must be considered tenuous. She tentatively posits that male incest victims are abused more often by males than by females and that both mother and father incest perpetrators tend to have emotional, social and psychological problems compounded by poor impulse control, low self-esteem and alcohol abuse.

James and Nasjleti (1983) in a report on their clinical experience with sexually abusive families, report that a minority of their cases involved female perpetrators. Although, the psychological profiles of these mothers are sketchy, in general they show signs of infantile and extreme dependency needs, a marriage relationship that is absent or emotionally empty, possessive and overprotective attitudes toward child victims, and alcohol used as a crutch. These perpetrators expect their children to meet their emotional needs and because of the mother's traditional role as a caretaker, they are able to hide the sexually explosive nature of these contacts.

Chasnoff, Burns, Schnoll, Burns, Chisum, and Kyle-Sproe (1986) reported on three cases of sexual abuse by a mother of her infant. The mothers all were separated from their sexual partners, had demonstrated symptoms of confusion regarding sexual identity, and had sought assistance with chemical dependency during pregnancy. Two of the three were diagnosed as suffering from borderline personality disorder and two had been raped. All three women were isolated in their living arrangements and the authors believe that the sexual abuse was motivated by loneliness. The social alienation and isolation of the mothers were significant facts in the molestation of their infants.

Goodwin and DiVasto (1989) reviewed six reported cases of incest involving mother perpetrators and daughter victims as well as two cases of grandmother-granddaughter incest. These cases deviate from the usual descriptions of incest and the authors note that physical closeness between mothers and daughters is less subject to taboo than are father and daughter contact. The greater toleration of physical intimacy between mothers and daughters makes it more difficult for the child, the parent, and eventually the therapist to recognize when contact between the perpetrator and the victim become incestuous. Although Goodwin and DiVasto acknowledged that since the reports of mother-daughter incest are few and brief, and any conclusions must be tentative, they find that the mothers seem to be similar to those mothers who perpetrate mother-son incest. They describe the mothers as aggressive women who have abandoned their maternal role for an exploitive relationship with their children. Their need for nurturance precipitates a sexual relationship with the child. In all cases of mother-daughter incest, the mothers were involved in deteriorating marriages. Goodwin and DiVasto believe that mother-daughter incest is more common than the rare case reports suggest.

Kempe and Kempe (1984) suggested that with the increased divorce rate, an increasing number of boys are living alone with their mothers. These boys may become a source of comfort and closeness, which may sometimes substitute for the companionship previously experienced in marriage. Although this in itself is normal, it can lead to problem behaviors, such as the mother taking the boy to bed for comfort. Kempe and Kempe note that society is more ready to believe that there is a sexual aspect to fathers who sleep with daughters as compared to mothers who sleep with sons. They describe two case studies in which sleeping arrangements also included overt sexual behavior and state the psychological effects to the boy can be devastating.

Krug (1989) reported on eight histories of men who were sexually abused by their mothers as children. In these cases, seven of the mothers slept with their sons regularly until the boys were teenagers. The mother perpetrators, who were either divorced or had troubled marriages, appeared to want to satisfy emotional and relational needs through their sons. Some were clearly socially insecure and isolated. In four of the incidents, the mothers initiated actual sexual contact; in the others, there was no overt sexual behavior. None of these perpetrators were described as psychotic.

In an article that described different types of incest, Lukianowicz (1972) discussed five cases of female perpetrators--three mother-son and two aunt-nephew. In one incident of mother-son incest, the mother was a widow; in the second, the mother's married life was very unhappy. Both of these perpetrators became very dependent on their eldest sons, in whom they saw the idealized young lovers of their own youth. The third mother was a chronic schizophrenic of low intelligence. One of the aunts was hypomanic and seduced her nephew during a manic phase; the other aunt was generally promiscuous. Lukianowicz reported that in many of the incidents studied, social isolation was a very important etiological factor.

Several conclusions can be made from the research on female perpetrators:

1. Awareness about women perpetrators of sexual abuse has, in recent years, greatly increased. However,

sexual contact between children and women is a minority of child-adult sexual contacts; the traditional view of child sexual abuse as instigated by primarily male perpetrators is correct.

2. Child sexual abuse by females does, however, occur and is probably not as rare as earlier literature indicates.

3. The range is great in the estimated frequency of sexual abuse cases in which women are perpetrators; different studies and the definition of sexual abuse used, sample selected, and methodology employed must be considered.

4. Female sexual abusers whose victims are children are less likely than men to fit the psychiatric definition of "pedophile."

5. There are many different circumstances in which females may engage in child sexual abuse. The circumstances that lead women to sexually abuse children can often be differentiated from those causing men to do so. One such example is sexual abuse which occurs in conjunction with a dominant male and in which the woman plays a secondary role.

6. Many studies depict women who sexually abuse children as being loners, socially isolated, alienated, likely to have had abusive childhoods, and apt to have emotional problems. However, most are not psychotic.

Based on the researcher's experience of evaluating and treating women perpetrators, the data suggests an additional theoretical construct that may account for some of the instances of actual sexual abuse by women. This suggested conceptualization is based upon a case study approach. The methodology of single case study material can be used in the beginning stages of a research effort. Case studies can provide a basis for the development of theory and hypotheses, which can then be subjected to a controlled experimental approach (Fantuzzo and Twentyman, 1986; Plotkin, Azar, Twentyman, and Perri, 1981). The following case studies are specific instances in which they propose that a significant loss experienced by the women created vulnerability and a readiness to become involved in sexual abuse of a child.

The profile of a female perpetrator researchers have observed is a woman whose history of losses along with a lack of healthy, secure relationships during childhood prompts her to cross the delicate line of caretaker and nurturer to sexual abuser. This woman is not psychotic but is apt to be insecure and emotionally isolated. Thus the sexually abusive behavior is triggered by a particular loss; the relationship between the female perpetrator and the victim is emotional as well as sexual and appears to attempt to primarily satisfy the woman's emotional needs. In my experience in working with male survivors, the profile of this type female perpetrator does not necessarily include the loss of her marriage, but the loss of the relationship. Her husband may pay little attention to her. He might be having an affair, or spend an inordinate amount of time away from home with activities or work.

While empirical research data to support this hypothesis is not yet available, there are a number of studies that demonstrate a relationship between a mother's experience of stress and a heightened risk or potential for child abuse. Holden, Kosisky, Willis, and Foltz (1990) report significantly higher scores on the Child Abuse Potential instrument and higher levels of stress on the Parent Stress Index for mothers who were in a treatment program for abusing children. Nicholas and Bieber (1990) reported their findings that male and female college students who gave retrospective accounts of sexual abuse reported higher sexual abuse by fathers than by mothers, but did not display other significant effects. However, mothers were reported as acting more overprotective than fathers. Santrock, Warshak, and Elliott (1982) suggest the possibility that in the case of divorce a child of the opposite sex may become a substitute for the now absent spouse. This sometimes leads to a smothering, overly nurturant relationship that may slide into emotional or sexual abuse. These researchers also suggest from their observations of child-stepmother interactions that a remarriage of the biological father and the advent of a stepmother is more difficult and conflicting for boys than for girls.

These studies are representative of the many efforts to locate regularities in the interactions between parents and children and the occurrence of abuse. The research indicates that stress is a significant factor; mothers who are abusing children often display stressful life experiences that may precipitate abusive acts. Researchers Dohrenwend and Shrout (1985) reported under the impact of a significant emotional loss, a woman may be more needy, less controlled, and more responsive to a relationship which can be rationalized as affectionate and positive. When considering environmental stimuli, opportunity, and availability of a child, a woman may progress in a gradual step-by-step movement into a full-fledged sexual exploitation of a child.

According to Finkelhor (Finkelhor, 1984; Araji and Finkelhor, 1985) there are four components that contribute, in differing degrees and forms, to development of a child molester's behavior. To explain the diversity of behavior of sexual abusers, there are four factors in a complementary process. These four factors are sexual arousal, emotional congruence, blockage, and disinhibition:

Sexual arousal: In order for an adult to be aroused by a child, there has frequently been cultural or familial conditioning to sexual activity with children or early fantasy reinforced by masturbation.

Emotional congruence: There is comfort in relating to a child and satisfaction of emotional need through the abuse. This is apt to be due to arrested development through limited intelligence, immaturity or low self-esteem.

Blockage: Age appropriate sexual opportunities may be blocked by bad experiences with age appropriate adults, sexual dysfunction, limited social skills, or marital disturbance.

Disinhibition: The abuser may lose control through impulse control deficits, psychosis, alcohol, drugs, stress, or nonexistent family rules.

Finkelhor suggests that examination of these factors can help explain why sexual abusers are predominately male. Rowan, Rowan, and Langelier (1981) studied 600 sex offender evaluations in New Hampshire and Vermont and found that in only nine cases (1.5 percent) was the perpetrator a woman. These nine incidents are reviewed in terms of Finkelhor's (1984) four-factor model. In five of the incidents studied, the abuse occurred in conjunction with a dominant male partner; in four, the woman acted independently. The histories of several of the women revealed a history of childhood abuse and all had serious psychological problems or limited intelligence. The victims of the four women who acted independently were male. Of the five women who acted in conjunction with a male, three victimized females, one victimized a male, and one victimized both a son and a daughter. The authors concluded that none of these incidents were true paraphilics according to the DSM-lll-R but that the female molesters did fit the model proposed by Finkelhor.

Understanding what motivates a person to abuse children sexually does NOT excuse him or her, or remove responsibility for the choices he or she has made. Although potentially abused as a child, the perpetrator is still responsible for his adult behavior and for the denial system that allows the abuse to continue. The adult is responsible for protecting the welfare of children; therefore, the adult is responsible for protecting children even from himself or herself if necessary.

The focus of sexual abuse may pass from daughter to daughter, or child to child, as each outgrows his or her availability or desirability. A sexual abuse perpetrator's victims may include only relatives, or he may abuse other children he comes in contact with as well. Many perpetrators do not discriminate based on gender. Some perpetrators will violate anyone with whom they have access. He may pursue activities or professions that allow him access to children, such as teaching, pediatrics, child care giving, scout leading, little league coaching, recreation activity leading, etc.

My clients often report situations where several family members have been victimized by the same perpetrator. Survivors subsequently struggle with the decision whether to restrict their children's contact with the family member who abused them. Some survivors cease all contact with their perpetrators. Other survivors allow their children only supervised contact with the perpetrator, while they maintain distance. The latter has many implications because sexual abuse can occur even with lack of physical contact between the perpetrator and the child.

Sexual abuse perpetrators may restrain themselves for periods of time, but they are unable to stop themselves from abusing again. They do not stop at one incident. Russell's research revealed that in 48 percent of the incidents studied, the child had been abused between two and twenty times. In 10 percent of the incidents, the abuse had taken place more than 20 times. For the child, it often becomes an ongoing childhood experience, stopping only when the child runs away, or leaves home for college or to live on their own. Studies on runaway children reveal that the majority of runaways were driven out of their homes by physical or sexual abuse. For these victims, the danger at home seemed far worse than the potential danger on the streets. Those who rescue runaways know that if they do not rescue the child within a few days the probability the child will be killed is very high, a casualty of the streets sought as refuge. This is a sad commentary for the child who ran away thinking the streets were safer than what they experienced at home.

Is Recovery Possible?

After reviewing countless stories on sexual abuse and incest recovery, I have come to the conclusion that recovery requires a multifaceted therapeutic process in conjunction with: self-help groups, support groups, group therapy, and workshops.

No two survivors follow the same journey to recovery. However, it is abundantly clear all recovered survivors work extremely long and diligently to regain their self-esteem, motivation and power to become the person they were born to be. Fortunately for their sake and the sake of generations to come, they have had the strength and courage to begin the healing process and endure the rocky road to recovery.

Focusing on Prevention

We can educate children to protect themselves. Parents cannot merely tell a child to say "no" to strangers. Furthermore, it is often too late to wait until it is time to talk about the birds and the bees. Although some children are abused before their first birthday, most perpetrators do not abuse children until after they begin to walk and talk, still others do not abuse children until the onset of puberty.

Parents need to empower their children and support them in the ownership of their bodies and their lives. This begins the moment the child is handed to them in the delivery room. Do not mistake this empowerment to mean the child is to be held responsible for stopping sexual abuse. The child needs your guidance and support to learn that he or she owns his or her body and that no one is ever allowed to touch him or her in ways she or he does not like. The child needs to know you believe him or her and that you will support him or her in this regard.

Most importantly for the safety of children, women need to accept the reality that men constitute the majority of sexual abusers of children; women need to be aware of the men they chose as partners. Judith Herman, M.D., author of *Father-Daughter Incest*, stated: "As in the case with other crimes against women and children, for too long the power of the justice system has protected the men who victimized them...As long as the justice system remains a male preserve, it can hardly be expected to reform itself . . . The initiative for those reforms that have already been carried out has come almost entirely from women: from the rape counselor, the child advocate, and the small minority of women who work within the system--we look forward to a time when women, who are so frequently the victims and rarely the offenders, adjudicate the majority of domestic and sexual crimes."

Chapter Three

Sexual Abuse and Incest Defined

Traditionally, incest was defined as "sexual intercourse between two persons too closely related to marry legally-- sex between siblings, first cousins, the seduction by fathers of their daughters." This dysfunctional blood relationship, however, does not completely describe what children are experiencing. To fully understand all sexual abuse, we need to look beyond the blood bond and include the emotional bond between the victim and his or her perpetrator. Thus, a new definition has emerged. The new definition now relies less on the blood bond between the victim and the perpetrator and more on the experience of the child.

"Incest is both sexual abuse and an abuse of power. It is violence that does not require force. Another is using the victim, treating them in a way that they do not want or in a way that is not appropriate by a person with whom a different relationship is required. It is abuse because it does not take into consideration the needs or wishes of the child; rather, it meets the needs of the other person at the child's expense. If the experience has sexual meaning for another person, in lieu of a nurturing purpose for the benefit of the child, it is abuse. If it is unwanted or inappropriate for her age or the relationship, it is abuse. Incest [sexual abuse] can occur through words, sounds, or even exposure of the child to sights or acts that are sexual but do not involve her. If she is forced to see what she does not want to see, for instance, by an exhibitionist, it is abuse. If a child is forced into an experience that is sexual in content or overtone that is abuse. As long as the child is induced into sexual activity with someone who is in a position of greater power, whether that power is derived through the perpetrator's age, size, status, or relationship, the act is abusive. A child who cannot refuse, or who believes she or he cannot refuse, is a child who has been violated." (E. Sue Blume, *Secret Survivors*).

Sexual abuse can be as subtle (covert) as any person showing pornographic pictures or movies to a child. It is any man hugging a child while pressing his hard penis against her. It is anyone consistently invading a child's privacy, such as entering the bathroom or bedroom without knocking, catching her unaware and indisposed. It is "playfully" pulling her swimsuit bottom down in the pool or pulling her panties down without her permission. Sexual abuse is anyone bathing the child when the child is old enough to bathe herself. It is any person who touches or caresses the child in ways she does not like or in ways that are sexual. It is any man holding a child on his lap when he has an erection. It is any trusted adult who stares at or makes comments about the child's body. It is anyone kissing the child in a way that is sexual for the giver. It is seemingly innocuous touching, wrestling, tickling, or playing which has sexual overtones or meaning for the other person.

Sexual abuse is as blatant (overt) as instructing or asking the child to lie in bed in an intimate position, fondling, digital, penis or object penetration of the rectum or vagina, or instructing a child to perform oral sex or performing oral sex on the child. It is forcing the child to touch others or be touched by others, including other children.

Overt sexual abuse is openly sexual and apparent. Although there may be an attempt to deny that it is abusive, there is no attempt to hide the fact that it is sexual in nature. Covert sexual abuse is more insidious. Thus, identifying it is harder, because the sexual nature of the action is disguised. The perpetrator acts as if she or he is doing something non-sexual, when in fact he or she is being sexual. The betrayal then becomes two-fold. The child is not only abused, but also tricked or deceived about the act. In this dishonesty, the child is unable to identify or clarify his or her perception of the experience. The unreal or surreal sense that accompanies any sexual abuse is intensified when the child is tricked into disbelief. Thus, the child doubts his or her perceptions and feelings and believes that there is something wrong with himself or herself because he or she feels terrible. To make matters worse, everyone around her acts as if nothing is wrong. Thus, she feels crazy, as if she is the one with the problem.

Without "validation" for her feelings or perceptions, the victim is again victimized.

Another destructive dynamic in covert sexual abuse or incest occurs when the adult treats the child as a pseudo or surrogate spouse. The child is treated like an equal, and a peer, rather than as a child. Although the dynamic is non-sexual, "the child is being used by another, treated in a way that is not wanted or not appropriate by a person with whom a different relationship is required."

In summary, sexual abuse or incest includes any of the following behaviors:

- An adult or older child sexually or erotically contacting, touching, fondling.
- Instructing the child to touch an adult or child in sexual or erotic areas.
- Any touch that is sexual for the giver.
- Putting objects in the child's vagina or rectum.
- Digital penetration of the vagina or rectum.
- Oral sex.
- Unnecessary or prolonged washing of the child's genital area.
- Bathing the child when they are old enough to bathe themselves.
- Photographing the child nude or in sexually provocative poses.
- Sexualized conversation.
- Showing the child pornographic materials or having them in areas which are easily accessible and viewed by the child.

- Making fun or ridiculing the child's sexual development or sexuality (i.e. sissy, woos, motherfucker, faggot, prick, cocksucker, whore, cunt, cry baby, flat chested, two fried eggs, little dick, wiener, etc.).
- Comparing one child's penis or breasts with another child or adult.
- An adult or older child exposing his or her genitals to the child.
- Masturbating when the child can see such activity.
- Any act of being sexual or seductive to the child or when the child can observe such activity between others.
- Allowing the child to observe adults or older children bathing or getting dressed as a routine experience.
- Showering or bathing with the child.
- Voyeurism.
- Overly rigid rules on dress.
- Adults wearing excessively revealing clothes—wearing only slip, panties, and bra or shorts, or robe which doesn't adequately cover the genital area.
- Walking around nude in front of the child.
- Forcing the child to remove clothes before being hit or spanked.
- Verbal and emotional abuse that has sexual overtones.
- Forcing the child to be sexual with animals.
- Forcing the child into prostitution.
- Forcing the child to witness others being sexually abused.

You may think this list describing behavior considered sexual abuse is preposterous. Or that most would not cause harm to the child. However, I assure you, I have heard each one of these and worse from many men and women independent of the other, who have suffered significantly from these experiences. This list has been compiled from the experiences of men and women who suffer the aftereffects based on the new definition of sexual abuse or incest.

Bathing or showering with children as young as infants, I learned, is common in many families. The most frequent rationale for parents to have their children bathe or shower with them is "saving time." While this practice may not cause any harm to your child because you have no "sexual intent," it does, however, set the precedent for the child to experience taking a bath or shower as acceptable behavior with a trusted adult. Therein lies the danger. The most frequent tactics a perpetrator employs to gain a child's trust and acceptance is behavior and activities the child will feel comfortable with and not suspect as something "strange." If the child is accustomed to this practice with the parent, she or he will be amenable to bathing or showering with any trusted adult--that trusted adult could be a perpetrator.

Furthermore, clients who remember bathing/showering with their parents recall feeling uncomfortable or embarrassed by the close proximity of their parent's nude body, particularly the penis, scrotum, and pubic hair, which could be the same height as the child's face. When the mother holds her child, the child is held against the bare breast(s). This too is reported as being an uncomfortable or embarrassing experience for the child.

A client recalled an incident with a friend's 4-year-old daughter, Katie, who routinely took showers with her father. A longtime male friend of this family came to visit. After he entered the bathroom to take a shower, Katie stripped her clothes off and asked to be let into the locked bathroom--she wanted to take a shower with him. This mother did not expect this behavior from her daughter. She believed her daughter would understand this was an activity between family members only.

Another client remembers her sexual abuse between age 8 and 9 by her maternal grandfather. She recalls, "He invited me into the shower with him. I remember him soaping me all over, quite different from what I remember my mother doing--an activity she had long ago stopped because I was a 'big girl.' It felt strange somehow, but he was my grandfather and I loved him. Each time he rubbed me with soap I felt a sensation I had never felt before--it was both pleasurable and sickening. Then one day he took a shower without inviting me. I felt hurt, confused and rejected. I didn't know what I had done to make him mad. Then a few days later he asked me again and our old familiar routine was back in place. I felt relieved and confused, because the pleasurable and sickening feeling was there too. There were many times he didn't invite me and I would feel hurt, confused and rejected, then he would invite me again, and I would feel the relief. As an adult looking back, I realize the times he didn't invite me were when one or both my parents were home. He also showed me how to 'soap' his penis. After my tenth birthday I stopped going into the shower with him--something clicked in my head--'I don't like this,' and I refused to come with him when he invited me. He seemed to accept this without reprisal."

You might think I am overreacting to the practice of bathing or showering with children, because you know you have no "sexual intent" and your child would never be around anyone who is a perpetrator. While this may be the case, I urge you to consider that the most remote possibility that your child could be vulnerable to a perpetrator is well worth your ceasing or not engaging in this practice. If I wanted to tell every story I have heard about how perpetrators within the family or family friends have sexually abused a child while the parents are at home, I would need to write another book.

In listening to many stories of sexual abuse and incest, I have discovered that a child is rarely subjected to only one type of sexual abuse. After working with sexual abuse survivors for over fifteen years, I have learned the sad truth about the human mind's ability to seemingly conceive of endless ways to sexually abuse children.

Aftereffects of Sexual Abuse and Incest

The definition of sexual abuse and incest states that sexual abuse and incest are more than sexual acts--they affect all aspects of the survivor's life. The manifestation of sexual abuse and incest take many forms of abuse that occur during childhood. There are the violence and violation of physical abuse, the self-esteem consequences of emotional abuse, and often the actual or perceived abandonment of the non-perpetrator(s) or parent(s) and the confusion and chaos caused within a dysfunctional family environment. Sexual abuse is the most devastating form of abuse a child can endure. It robs the child of a childhood, of innocence, of ownership of his or her body, and of the potential for his or her healthy sexual development. It damages trust and disrupts bonding. It isolates the child in an unpredictable, emotionally confusing bond with the perpetrator who has security through secrecy and threats. In short, sexual abuse and incest damages the child's mind, body and spirit.

Every aspect of the child's physical, emotional, mental, behavioral, sexual, and spiritual self is compromised. The capacity for the child to relate in healthy ways is affected. Although there are common denominators within the various aspects of the effects of sexual abuse, I will address each separately.

PHYSICAL: The physical nature of sexual abuse seems clear, yet it is not. We believe when we see the child's body injured or maimed from sexual abuse, we can treat and account for the physical effects. Unless a therapeutic process specifically directed for sexual abuse or incest is completed, the survivor suffers on all levels throughout his or her life.

Some common physical aftereffects of sexual abuse are: alienation from the body--not accepting one's body image; failing to heed body signals or take care of one's body; manipulating body size to avoid sexual attention; difficulty in having intercourse or instigating vaginisums, which prevent penetration.

Sexual abuse can weaken survivors' immune systems according to Dr. Frank Putnam of the National Institute of Mental Health and Dr. Martin Teicher of Harvard Medical School. Putnam conducted studies on 170 girls, 6-15 years old--half had been sexually abused, half had not--for seven years. The abused girls displayed symptoms such as:

- abnormally high stress hormones, which can kill neurons in brain areas crucial for thinking and memory
- high levels of an antibody that weaken the immune system

Teicher completed a series of brain studies on 402 children and adults, many of whom had been sexually or physically abused. His findings revealed that sexual or physical abuse creates:

- arrested growth of the left hemisphere of the brain which can hamper development of language and logic
- growth of the right hemisphere of the brain (the site for emotion) at an abnormally early age

The result of a weakened immune system includes more profound as well as seldom recognized physical aftereffects such as: vaginal, ovarian, prostate, or breast cancer. Louise Hay in her book, *Heal Your Body--The Mental Causes for Physical Illness and the Metaphysical Way to Overcome Them*, stated:

"A few years ago, I was diagnosed as having cancer of the vagina. With my background of being raped when I was five years old and being a battered child, it was no wonder I had manifested cancer in the vaginal area. Having already been a teacher of healing for several years, I was very aware that I was now being given a chance to practice on myself and prove what I had been teaching others. Being aware that cancer comes from a pattern of deep resentment that is held for a long time, until it literally eats away at the body, I knew I had a lot of mental work to do. I immediately began to work with my own teacher to clear old patterns of resentment. Up to that time, I had not acknowledged that I harbored deep resentment. We are often so blind to our own patterns. A lot of forgiveness work was in order. The other thing I did was to go to a good nutritionist and completely detoxify my body. So between the mental and physical cleansing, in six months I was able to get the medical profession to agree with what I already knew; that I no longer had any form of cancer. I still keep the original lab report as a reminder of how negatively creative I could be."

Other physical aftereffects of sexual abuse/incest may include the following: gastrointestinal problems, gynecological disorders (may include spontaneous bleeding and vaginal infections), headaches, migraines, arthritis, joint pain, eating disorders, and alcohol or drug abuse.

Many studies and midwives' first-hand experiences have noted a high correlation between women who are sexual abuse survivors and women who require cesarean deliveries. The sexual abuse victim makes a gallant effort to prevent the rape by tightening her vaginal muscles. The tightening response often occurs even years later, such as in childbirth; in these incidents, a woman may be unable to relax her vaginal muscles, which is natural and necessary for a vaginal delivery. Fortunately, if midwives are made aware of prior sexual abuse, there are methods to assist in a vaginal delivery. If you are a survivor, be sure to inform your doctor or midwife. If your doctor does not know how to assist you in this regard, search until you find someone who does--It is worth the effort. Another profound aftereffect of sexual abuse and incest is self-injury. Karen Conterio, a Chicago-based consultant specializing in self-injury, along with Armando Favazzo, a psychiatrist, sent a survey to 1,250 people; 250 responded. The results were published in Community Mental Health Journal, "The Plight of Chronic Self-Mutilators." Self-injuring behavior refers to cutting, self-abuse, self-mutilation, para-suicide, and deliberate self-harm. The most common self-injuring behaviors are cutting, burning, breaking bones, pinching skin, ingesting, injecting and inserting foreign materials, interfering with the healing process of wounds, punching, slapping, picking skin, pulling hair, and bloodletting.

In the ten years I have worked with sexual abuse and incest survivors, the majority of my clients have exhibited one or more of these self-injuring behaviors before or during treatment. Survivors state that they are unable to accept or express uncomfortable or overwhelming feelings due to underlying emotional conflicts. They further state that physical pain is more manageable than emotional pain. Physical pain is tangible, while emotional pain is intangible. Physical wounds are obvious and can be attended to with observable results.

Ironically, physical wounds provide a distraction from the emotional pain. Furthermore, society overall responds with significant empathy when anyone is physically injured. However, society's response to emotional pain is quite different--one is told to "snap out of it," "quit your belly-aching," "you're making it up," "why are you bringing that up," "it happened [ten years] ago--forget it and move on." Other less obvious forms of self-injury are: hatred of the body, self-hatred, numbing feelings, guilt, and self-loathing.

Besides suffering the physical trauma, the survivor questions why she or he did not defend himself or herself. The victim often reasons that they were to blame because, perhaps, they had some desire for sexual contact. Frequently, survivors remember experiencing sexual pleasure; therefore, they blame themselves for the abuse. Perpetrators and society overall point to the fact that erection, ejaculation and orgasm are proof that the survivor must have wanted or enjoyed the sexual contact. Thus, the reasoning is that no actual abuse took place and, therefore, no treatment is needed. The survivor suffers in silence and seldom equates his or her pain and anguish with the sexual abuse that occurred long ago; to the victim, the effects of the abuse do not seem connected to present issues, or the act(s) or trauma has been forgotten.

Because the survivor believes her body has betrayed her, she hates her body. She "shuts herself off" from her body, seeing it as something ugly, unattractive and something she cannot trust will function as she deems. In some paradoxical way, victims see their bodies as having minds of their own--possessing powers or abilities that arouse sexual desire in others. Many survivors see their bodies as both distasteful and dangerous. A recently divorced 55-year-old male client, who was abused at age 10 by a 14-year-old girl, believed every woman was attracted to him and desired him sexually. He assumed that he and I would eventually be sexual. He was shocked to learn that I had no intention of being sexual and was not having difficulty at maintaining that boundary. He believed he could seduce any woman he wanted. He was disappointed to learn he did not have the power he thought he possessed and, simultaneously, was relieved he could maintain a non-sexual relationship with a woman he considered attractive.

Another physical aftereffect of sexual abuse is the tendency to be "accident-prone." This means the survivor does not pay attention to his or her body in relation to his or her surroundings and tends to bump into things or injure himself or herself by misjudging space between objects and their bodies. This phenomenon is prevalent with children who have been spanked.

Another form of unconscious physical injury is becoming a "daredevil" or participating in high-risk activities.

MENTAL: When the child's physical boundaries are violated, his or her mind is also violated. The insidious nature of the mental abuse can be explained by using the analogy of the reactions of a deer when its eyes are exposed to the headlights of an oncoming car. The deer becomes so disoriented by the blinding light that it jumps toward the car instead of away from it--so it is with the child who has been sexually abused. Once abused, the child believes his or her body is something that others control.

Frequently, survivors protect their psyche by way of a dissociative response. Survivors report they "left" their body or "checked out," "zoned out," so the abuse happened "to my body and not to me." The signs of a dissociative state are "freezing," "spacing out," difficulty with concentration (diagnosed as ADD), forgetting, staring, emotional numbness or unreality. All of these states hinder the person in achieving healthy, appropriate functioning.

Reality is defined by the perpetrator who uses many methods of distortion and deception. Frequently, the perpetrator tells the victim that what she or he thinks is happening is really not. Often, the abuse is ignored or even denied by everyone in the family. Anyone who dares to discuss the topic is told that they are crazy, that it never happened. The fairy tale, *The Emperor's New Clothes* has become the family dynamic. The survivor is subsequently labeled a "little liar," who cannot be trusted.

Another violation of the child that causes mental trauma is to blame the victim; this is done by convincing everyone (usually the mother) that the child "wanted" or allowed the sexual contact and enjoyed it.

Additionally, perpetrators often rename the abuse. The sexual activity is presented as a "game" and the perpetrator is "choosing" the child as his special play partner. Effects of this type of sexual violation cause the victim to place uncertainty and shame upon themselves; victims may wonder, "What is 'wrong' with me that I feel so 'bad,' and 'yucky,' when this is supposed to be fun and I was chosen because I am special."

Perpetrators use a plethora of explanations to justify the abuse; they tell the child such things as, "I am doing this so you will know what sex is about." A female client's father used sexual abuse as punishment for bad behavior. If she and her sister had sibling arguments, the punishment for her, the older of the two, was to perform oral sex on him. She explained, "How my mother did not know this was going on, I do not know. He took me into the family room, unzipped his pants and told me to take his penis in my mouth. I complied for fear of other more grave consequences."

No matter which justification technique is employed, the outcome remains the same--the child learns to distrust his or her own view of reality. Even more traumatic is when the abuse takes place after the child is asleep. Frequently, the child reasons and believes that his or her only defense is to lie still and act as if they are asleep, hoping the abuser will leave. Sometimes the child cries out, assuming the parent will stop because "they are being hurt."

In some circumstances, the abuser may act as if he or she is comforting the child after a bad dream. The child is then faced with a reality dilemma, "Did I dream it or did I experience what I think I experienced?" The abuser does not discuss it openly; if he does, the motive is to dissuade the child from believing the experience. This covert abuse is particularly powerful in convincing the child not to trust his or her thoughts and perceptions of the world.

As described in physical aftereffects, dissociation is a common response for survivors. Dissociation also affects mental aspects of sexual abuse and incest. Unfortunately, the dissociating response often continues into adulthood and many people dissociate, even in situations that are not abusive. This response keeps them emotionally distant and unable to achieve a high level of intimacy with others, or to function effectively at work. Frequently, people such as this are given labels, such as: "stupid," "air heads," "slow," "ADD," obsessive compulsive disorder, schizoaffective disorder, schizoid disorder of childhood or adolescence, schizoid personality disorder, or other schizophrenia types. In some incidents, survivors who use the dissociative response are diagnosed as mentally retarded. These same misdiagnoses are placed on children who have been physically punished.

One of the most damaging aspects of sexual abuse is the development of a "victim mentality." When a person is abused and then left to cope with it alone, they begin to form a defeatist belief about themselves and the world around them. The abused child sees the world around them as unsafe, unpredictable, dangerous, and uncontrollable. "No one can really be trusted," becomes their belief system. Furthermore, the victim has learned from being abused that what she or he thinks, feels, does, wants, or needs makes no difference. Although the abuse has stopped, he or she continues to perceive himself or herself as ineffective, powerless and worthless. A person with a "victim mentality" frequently asks questions such as, "Why?" "Why me?" "Why did this happen?" They conceptualize the abuse as, "happening" rather than "my mother or father hurt me," because the reality is too painful to accept. They perceive themselves as powerless to change anything, as was the case when they were abused. This belief system persists until the core wound from the abuse has been healed.

The "perpetrator mentality" is the most insidious aspect of the sexual abuse and/or incest trauma. While the "victim mentality" is one of self-blame, the "perpetrator mentality" is one of other-blame. These two debilitating mentalities fit together perfectly--the survivor believes she or he is to blame while the perpetrator believes the survivor is to blame. Even more disturbing is the fact many "perpetrator mentality" beliefs are accepted by overall society. The perpetrator leads himself to believe such things as: "The child seduced me." "I couldn't help myself." "What was she doing wearing only her panties in the living room?" He describes the child as a seductress. In other words, he is saying, "I can't control myself and it is [his/her] fault." *Playboy*, *Penthouse*, *Hustler*, et al, promote the "perpetrator mentality" under the protection of the freedom of speech act.

If the perpetrator does not blame other people for the abuse, he may blame circumstances for it. For example, parents often report crowded sleeping arrangements as reasons for the abuse. However, researcher S. K. Weinberg, *Incest Behavior*, 1955, reported that frequently when children were "forced" to sleep with a parent and were sexually abused, there were other alternatives and space limitation was merely an excuse to justify the behavior.

EMOTIONAL: The emotional aftereffects of sexual abuse and incest are very powerful. These emotions are so powerful that a survivor is afraid to be aware of them. Emotions include: Anger, rage, sadness, fear, guilt, loneliness, shame, and hurt. These emotions vary in intensity and duration. The fear of these emotions prompts the survivor to maintain a flat affect to "hold the pain at bay." Unfortunately, this flat affect keeps the survivor from experiencing life fully and from achieving intimacy in any relationship. Men generally need to learn that the expression of anger need not be associated with violence, nor the expression of sadness with weakness. Women generally need to learn to speak for themselves and to accept this assertion as a human right and not disguised aggression, as some want to label assertive behavior.

Nearly every sexual abuse or incest survivor incorporates shame as part of his or her identity. If this issue is not addressed, the survivor usually continues to self-abuse or to remain vulnerable to other's abuse and/or inappropriate authoritative behavior. Shame stems from neglectful or otherwise abusive relationships whereby the individual incorporates the belief she or he cannot be loved or accepted by anyone who truly knows him or her.

The case of Amy Fisher, the 16-year-old Long Island girl who was sexually abused by 35-year-old Joey Buttafuoco, is a classic example in which the perpetrator blames the survivor for seducing him. Buttafuoco contended she hung around his auto repair shop, acting in a way that was seductive and promiscuous, and he could not get away from her. Society further allows the perpetrator to portray himself as the misunderstood party in a society with "sexual hang-ups."

BEHAVIORAL: The behavioral aftereffect of sexual abuse or incest is very subtle. Men acting tough and aggressive and women acting weak and helpless are classic examples. The tougher the man acts is in exact correlation to his feelings of vulnerability, shame, guilt and weakness. The more weak and helpless the woman acts is in exact correlation to her feelings of vulnerability, guilt, shame and powerlessness. Sexual abuse or incest robs the person of a carefree childhood. Buried deep inside the survivor is a wounded child who needs acceptance and nurturing. As long as the survivor hates, ignores, denies, or fears that vulnerable, childlike aspect of themselves, their relationships remain superficial.

SPIRITUAL: The aftereffects to the sexual abuse victim's spirituality are profound, extensive and pervasive. It is a soul injury. Before the child has the opportunity to experience himself or herself as a fully functioning human being, they have been sexually abused. When they learn about God, they are taught that God protects us from harm. They often wonder such things as, "Why didn't he protect me?" Many religions also teach that God punishes those who are "bad." "I must be bad," the child reasons, "because God did not protect me. God must be punishing me for being bad. I am to blame. What did I do to deserve this?" Self-loathing and guilt ensues. Frequently, clients tell me they no longer believe in God. "If God was real, why did he let me be abused?" they ask. In order to fully heal, those who have turned away from their spirituality need to find a way to reconnect with their spiritual self.

SEXUAL: The aftereffects with respect to the survivor's sexuality are immediate. Humans are sexual beings from the moment of birth. The sexual abuse or incest survivor believes that their body does not belong to them. Their body is the ground on which this insidious battle took place. Touch is not experienced as affection, but as a violation for the survivor. Touch does not bond or reassure--it hurts and confuses the survivor.

E. Sue Blume in her book, *Secret Survivors*, writes, "Sex feels 'dirty,' and the survivor may have an aversion to being touched, especially in gynecological exams. Survivors frequently have a strong aversion to (or need for) particular sex acts; feeling betrayed by one's body; trouble integrating sexuality and emotionality; confusion or overlapping of affection, sex, dominance, aggression and violence. Sexuality is expressed through pursuing power in a sexual arena that is sexual acting out (self-abuse and manipulation, especially among women; abuse of others, especially among men); compulsively 'seductive' or compulsively asexual; must be sexual aggressor or cannot be; impersonal, 'promiscuous' sex with strangers concurrent with inability to have sex in intimate relationships (conflict between sex and caring); prostitute, stripper, 'sex symbol,' porn actress; sexual acting out to meet anger or revenge needs; 'sexaholism', avoidance; shutdown, crying after orgasm; all pursuit feels like violation; sexualizing of meaningful relationships; erotic response to abuse or anger; sexual fantasies of dominance or rape."

RELATING: The development of one's sense of self is ongoing. It is a journey, not a destination. Tragically, the sexual abuse or incest survivor's journey has been inexplicably contaminated. At the core of any healthy relationship is trust. Trust can be defined as a feeling of safety, comfort or security with another person. In healthy development, trust naturally evolves. The child cries to receive comfort, food or attention. As these cries for attention are attended to, the child learns to trust the caregiver.

As adults, how do we decide whether to trust? We share our thoughts and feelings with someone and watch their reaction; if the response feels safe, if it is caring, non-critical and non-abusive, the first step of trust has been established. For trust to grow, this positive response needs to become part of an ongoing and reliable pattern. It need not--nor can it be--perfect. For the survivor, trust has been skewed and betrayed, sometimes before she begins to walk and talk. Intimacy is impossible without trust; for the sexual abuse or incest survivor, trust is impossible--the inherent right to intimacy has been wrenched from their emotional grasp. The inherent right to intimacy and trust can be regained through the therapeutic process.

This distortion of intimacy teaches many confusing contradictions: to be cared about is to be taken from; to need someone puts one at risk of being taken advantage of; and to receive leads to an anticipated payback. For the sexual abuse or incest survivor, intimacy equals danger and damage. Intimacy has become more threatening than sex. As a survivor, she is accustomed to dealing with sex. She has learned the rules—"you get what you want at my expense"--and thus she detaches from her body and therefore is comfortable with the sexual interaction.

The survivor equates sex with love. After all, she was told by her perpetrator that he loved her while he was sexually abusing her. She believes that she is only accepted if she is willing to "give herself away." She can be sexual with strangers or friends, switching into automatic (even with her partner) as she did ever since the abuse, and feels nothing. Nevertheless, at some point in a serious relationship, she will begin to feel as if something has gone wrong.

Although she is starved for intimacy, she cannot experience it. She did not experience it as a child and, therefore, does not know how to have a healthy adult relationship. Nor does she know how to choose healthy men with whom to have a relationship. She will often reenact the abuse by choosing men who are verbal, physical or sexual abuse perpetrators. While she feels threatened or abused (without seeing a connection to her experience of sexual abuse or incest, if she remembers it) she is frequently unable to empower herself; thus, the power imbalance as occurred with her initial perpetrator is manifested again.

Power imbalances in relationships take several forms. Survivors frequently become involved in sexual relationships or marriage with older and/or more powerful people, simulating previous relationships with older, more powerful abusers. The sexual abuse survivor continues to be a "child." The survivor may connect with men who are strong and controlling "protectors" (caretaker, co-dependency) who may never abuse her, but with whom there is a basic power imbalance. In these circumstances, the victim has interpreted her partner's possessive control as attention or caring. Or she might see commitment as suffocation or engulfment. Intimacy means having to give everything away; she may avoid relationships out of fear she will be "sucked dry."

Underneath the fear of engulfment is the inherent need for intimacy. This inherent need for intimacy has been contaminated by the abuse and is now being experienced as acute fear of abandonment. This fear is compelling. She wants to control the actions and attitudes of her partner, requiring and demanding constant reassurance and contact. This constant demand compels the partner to withdraw. The relationship may be further complicated in incidents where the survivor chooses a partner who is unavailable. The pursuer and the withdrawer seem to find each other. Or perhaps they connect with each other because two pursuers recognize they would "overwhelm each other" with the constant intensity of pursuit before the relationship develops beyond the dating stage. On the other hand, the withdrawer finds the constant presence of another engulfing, seeking space in times of stress. The dance of "be close, don't be close," by the pursuer and withdrawer is a difficult balancing act.

Many survivors marry loving, attentive partners. However, ironically, the consistent love and attentiveness by the partner frequently becomes an enemy. For no apparent reason, the survivor may lose interest in sex or feel threatened or abused. She may suddenly think her partner is having an affair and may go to great lengths to catch him. This behavior puts a great strain on the relationship. Her partner may withdraw for emotional solace, unknowingly adding to the survivor's insecurities. She may even end the relationship believing he had an affair, only to repeat the pattern again.

The survivor desperately pursues sexual relationships, thinking that this will fill the emptiness. Survivors come to each new romance with tremendous need and no inner resources or skills to build an intimate relationship. Further, this combination--tremendous neediness and no inner resources or skills--results in dissatisfactory relationships. The fact is sex is not sex, and trust, caring and violation cannot co-exist.

Men face the same problems women survivors face with two exceptions--they judge themselves more harshly, and they have a very hard time recognizing they have been abused. Men's indoctrination since childhood dictates that they are to prove their sexual prowess. Sexual activity for boys as young as 12 is seldom considered inappropriate. Therefore, if an older girl initiates sex with a younger boy, he considers it an introduction to sex, proving his "manliness." Additionally, men are indoctrinated to defend themselves against all odds--to fight to the death to protect their manliness. They are expected to risk their life or sustain severe injury to protect their pride and self-respect. These distorted beliefs about "manliness" and "masculinity" are deeply ingrained and can lead to intense feelings of guilt, shame and inadequacy for the male survivor.

Both male and female survivors generally question whether they deserved or somehow wanted to be sexually abused; they believe if they failed to defend themselves, they must have wanted it. Although both female and male survivors frequently view their abuse as a loss of manhood or femininity and are disgusted with themselves for not "fighting back," men judge themselves more harshly.

As a result of their guilt, shame and anger, both men and women punish themselves by engaging in self-destructive behavior such as: alcohol or drug use, prostitution, rape and numerous other criminal behaviors. For some men self-destructive behavior means engaging in aggressiveness, such as road rage, arguing with friends or co-workers, or picking fights with strangers, as well as domestic violence as a way to regain their honor. Both men and women pull back from intimacy and end up feeling more and more isolated.

In summary: the legacy of every unhealed sexual abuse survivor includes diminished self-worth, limited ability to trust, and the burden of a shameful secret she or he cannot express. This legacy leaves the survivor's ability to develop necessary social contacts inhibited. She remains co-dependent on her caretakers--her nuclear or extended family, foster parents or her surrogate family, babysitter, doctor or priest--who are frequently her abusers.

Tragically, once she has been abused, other perpetrators recognize her vulnerability and she will become victim to another abuser. She is left with the tremendous conflict of--feeling a need to "keep her guard up" while never "needing anyone"; simultaneously, the festering wound of the abuse and neglect forces her desperation to "fill it." The conflicting messages in her childhood were not, "Come here and I will abuse you," but, "Come here because I love you and I want to show affection"; she was deceived, and the affection she expected was in fact abuse. Thus, the expected affection can no longer be trusted. She has learned that the appearance of love is something quite different, and she cannot trust it or feel safe.

Chapter Four

Why Self-Protection?

We generally teach girls to be passive and reward them for doing so. Girls are raised to be quiet, sweet and pretty; they are never to make a "scene." Boys are taught, expected and praised to be tough and self-assured, even at times when something troubles them. Whenever a person is traumatized, he or she resorts to familiar behavior; for girls this behavior usually means passivity while boys usually "tough it out"--thinking if they are strong and unemotional, no harm can occur.

Self-protection offers a direct and effective way to empower children to help themselves. Since the perpetrator cunningly and with forethought sets the stage to perpetrate this crime in secrecy, who is better able than the child to protect himself or herself? Perpetrators say they can sense a child to victimize; they sense this by the child's demeanor, body language and facial expressions. They sense the fear, the helplessness and the passivity. Perpetrators choose victims who they assume will keep the secret. No child needs to fall prey to these cunning predators.

Without knowledge of and permission to exercise self-protection, the only defense a child has against any kind of abuse is to accept the blame. A child cannot conceive the idea, "My father, uncle, mother, grandpa, grandma, aunt, brother, sister, cousin, friend, teacher, or baby-sitter is sick." Therefore, the only way to survive sexual abuse or incest is to assume that it is her fault. As a child, she has unquestioning trust for everyone. "Daddy, grandpa, uncle, cousin is good; it must be me." More important, she wants and needs her family to be a family. She believes she stabilizes and holds the family together. Therefore, she accepts an inappropriate role. Her needs are not being met; she is meeting the needs of everyone else at the expense of her own needs.

Tragically, many survivors believe they are the only one being abused. "I thought I was the only one. I thought if I let him abuse me he would not abuse my sister." This is rarely the case. Perpetrators usually abuse more than one child and frequently abuse several children during a given period.

Armed with this knowledge, it is imperative to teach children to protect themselves. However, protection techniques offer no guarantee. Teaching children: (1) good body image, (2) boundary setting, (3) fostering their self-esteem, and (4) not keeping secrets for others, can prevent abuse or prevent the same person from repeating the abuse.

Why Self-Protection?

Although techniques for self-protection are best initiated when the child begins to talk, it is imperative that your child is taught self-protection at any age. I have presented the techniques of self-protection in their simplest form to teach children beginning by the age 2 or 2 ½. You can modify the teaching of each technique according to your child's age. However, it is critical all concepts of self-protection are taught, practiced and reinforced continuously throughout childhood.

Chapter Five

What To Do--Spanking and Boundaries

At birth we intuitively know our bodies are sacred. This provides a built-in protection system. When we are startled by an uncomfortable noise or touch, this protective system kicks in. When a child squirms or throws both arms across the chest, the child is using this protective mechanism. Observers of child development refer to this self-protective mechanism as "startle response." Within a few hours of birth this startle response is apparent.

Adults need to respect children's sacred physical boundaries and inherent likes and dislikes beginning at birth. Lack of respect for a child can disturb a child's protection responses, rendering their intuitive perception of unwanted or uncomfortable touch to be either inoperative or very weak.

Parents can avoid thwarting this protection system by minimizing any touch or maneuvering that the child dislikes. When your child protests, you need to stop immediately and find an alternative approach. Immediately comfort the child by hugging and talking soothingly, such as, "I am sorry, there, there, I know it is uncomfortable." If the child is 2 years old and the protesting continues, the message the child is sending may be, "I want to do it myself." Children can learn to dress, undress and bathe themselves by age 2 or two-and-a-half with minimal help.

Yes, the fostering and development of this protective system takes time. However, remember the goal is to reinforce your child's right to protest uncomfortable or unwanted touch for any reason, rather than getting them dressed, undressed or into the bath quickly.

Comforting reinforces and validates the child's inherent perception: "My body is sacred and I have the right to protest." Comforting reinforces the child's inherent perception of comfortable or uncomfortable touch. Comforting also reinforces the child's right to protect their physical boundaries, which they will carry with them far after the time in which they require constant supervision.

Lack of comforting negates or discounts the child's perceptions, setting the stage for the child to allow themselves to be discounted and negated in other ways. Respecting a child's perception of acceptable or unacceptable touch based on their unique likes and dislikes (not based on yours) builds a deep level of self-protection into a child's psyche.

Ultimately, you have responsibility to protect the child's physical boundaries when the child is unable to gain cooperation and respect from others. For example, if anyone--including either parent, grandparent or any trusted adult--is playing and the child protests, interceding is important to stop the unwanted touch or play activity. This validates the child's perception that something is uncomfortable and protesting is an acceptable response.

Have you witnessed a child wincing when he or she is told or coaxed to kiss a friend or family member? It is obvious the child does not want to kiss or be kissed; however, the child is forced to act against his or her will. Furthermore, kissing a child on the mouth is inappropriate. For example, as adults, we do not kiss everyone we know on the mouth. Why, then, would a child want to be kissed on the mouth?

Have you seen an adult pinch a child on the cheek and make endearing comments--"Isn't she a little cutie?"-- grabbing the child, hugging her while she is wincing, whining or pushing to get away? These acts are all boundary violations. Forced compliance sets the stage for future boundary violation and abuse. More importantly, it also conveys the message that the child's dislikes are invalid, unimportant or wrong, and the child learns not to trust their own perceptions.

Interceding unwanted touch or play reinforces the child's intuitive perception that, "My body is sacred, and no one has the right to do things that are uncomfortable. Someone will intercede in my behalf."

The worst type of sacred boundary violation is the use of spanking as a form of discipline. Spanking, defined as slapping of the buttocks, is a form of hitting and is physical violence. This fact alone is reason enough to make the spanking of children unacceptable by the same standards that protect adults, who are not as vulnerable. However, there is more to spanking than simple hitting. Spanking also trespasses on one of the body's most private and sexual areas--the genitals. Furthermore, violent socialization of infants, children and youth by means of "spanking," "bopping," "switching," "licking," "whipping," "paddling," "popping," "whacking," "thumping," etc., conditions children to accept and tolerate aggression and violence. This leaves the child prey to sexual abuse and incest perpetrators. To address the inappropriateness of spanking children completely, we need to consider not only the issue of physical violence, but also the issue of sexual trespass.

As will be discussed in more detail in the section on appropriate suspicion, perpetrators target children who appear to have been victims before (quiet, withdrawn, compliant). A previous victim of sexual abuse tends to be quiet, easy to manipulate and more likely to comply with a perpetrator's request(s).

The harm of spanking to reinforce appropriate behavior has been thoroughly explained and demonstrated over the past century in a vast body of academic literature, scientific research, legal treatises, and recently in the popular media. Sexual consequences of spanking are rarely defined or discussed.

Like women's breasts, the buttocks are sexual or erogenous parts of the human anatomy, though not sex organs. Baring one's buttocks in public is considered indecent and unlawful. Exposure of buttocks in movies or on television is considered nudity. Anyone who fondles another person's buttocks without consent can lawfully be considered a sexual offender suspect. The sexual nature of the buttocks is determined not only by their proximity to the genitals, but also by their high concentration of nerve endings that lead directly to sexual nerve centers. Thus, the buttocks are a major center through which sexual signals can be transmitted.

The sexuality of the buttocks is significant not only to adults, but to children as well. Although children are sexually immature and void of active sex drives, they are neurological sexual beings who can experience erotic sensation at birth.

Since children are sexual beings and since the buttocks are in the sexual region of the body, we need to question the propriety of "spanking," "slapping," etc., children's buttocks. We generally understand that fondling or caressing a child's buttocks is a sexual offense (albeit the child may not understand it to be so). We also know that slapping an adult's buttocks is a sexual offense (even if the offender does not gain sexual pleasure from doing so).

Why is hitting or slapping a child's buttock not considered a sexual offense? A plausible explanation for this logic is simply that the majority of people are unable or unwilling to believe there could be anything indecent about a practice as old, common and accepted as the spanking of children; a "disciplinary measure" that nearly everyone has been exposed to in some form, at least once.

Even without sexual motives by the perpetrator, spanking can interfere with a child's normal sexual and psychological development. Because the buttocks are so close to the genitals and so multiply linked to sexual nerve centers, slapping them can trigger powerful and involuntary sensations of sexual pleasure. These sensations can occur even in very young children, and even in spite of great, clearly upsetting pain.

This kind of sexual stimulation, which undermines any disciplinary purpose and which most people would agree is unsuitable for children in any context, can cause a child to impressionably attach his or her sexuality to the idea of spanking. A child may also react against these unseemly feelings of pleasure by repressing his or her sexuality. A child such as this may have difficulty experiencing sexual pleasure and intimacy later in life.

An additional danger of spanking is the confusing mixture of pleasure with pain, which may become the basis for permanent sadomasochistic tendencies. Sadomasochism, in which a person takes pleasure in inflicting or receiving pain, drives behavior that is destructive to oneself and to others. While the intensity and background of an individual's tendencies toward sadomasochism vary widely, most studied incidents point to a single origin: childhood experiences of physical discipline or abuse including, "whipping, spanking, smacking, bopping, whacking, paddling, etc.," usually on the buttocks.

Many adults are sexually excited by spanking--sadomasochism (derivation of pleasure via inflicting physical or mental pain on oneself or others) and by flagellantism (responding sexually to being beaten or beating another person). While many flagellants seek to engage in consensual spanking between adults, some find the spanking of minors to be either more arousing or more opportune.

Since children up to 18 years can be, in some states, legally and forcibly spanked by parents, guardians, teachers, school principals and other childcare professionals, it is often easy for flagellants to obtain positions where they can sexually abuse children with almost no fear of repercussions. As long as parents see spanking as a legitimate act of discipline, and as long as the spanked child is presumed to have "deserved" it, sexually abusive spankers have an effective, moralistic disguise for their true motives.

Some parents rationalize spanking by saying, "Well, I know my intentions are purely non-sexual, so there is nothing wrong with my spanking my child." The problem with this rationale is that it fails to consider that children are at the mercy of other adults. Among these adults will always be someone with a motive of sexual abuse--albeit the perpetrator does not conceive it as such. Even spankings without a sexual motive contribute to the cover that sexually abusive spankers depend on, affirming the old excuse: "Hey, many people spank their children. What is the big deal, a good 'whack' never hurt anybody. My parents hit me and I turned out okay." However, many physical and emotional problems can be traced to the onset of physical punishment.

In my discussions with people who use spanking to promote compliance with instructions, the most frequent rationalization is that a 2-year-old child cannot be reasoned with--so spanking is the best alternative. When I then ask the adult if I can hit them because they cannot be reasoned with regarding hitting or spanking children, they are chagrined by the obvious analogy.

Another classic rationalization is the need to spank in emergency situations--when there is no time for explanations. An example of the rationalization that is frequently given is: "What if my child walks into the street with oncoming traffic. In this situation, one has to impress on the child that walking into the street is dangerous," they reason, "and spanking the child is the most effective alternative." This reasoning is faulty because spanking creates shock, whereby the mind is unable to focus or retain logic rather than enhance comprehension. Furthermore, hitting engenders rage rather than respect. Thus, instead of creating learning and compliance to avoid stepping into the street, the child has learned to distrust adults. In order to maintain the relationship, the child pushes the rage deep into the psyche; the accompanying response to body boundary violations is to act out in other ways that may include rebellion, violence, self-destructive behavior, etc.

Some people believe spanking is justified or even commanded in the *Bible*, specifically the book of *Proverbs*. There is a distinction, however, which is of key interest to fundamentalists, between the practice in King Solomon's day of beating people on the back and the modern American habit of buttocks hitting: the latter is not prescribed anywhere in the *Bible*. Furthermore, it needs to be pointed out that the *Old Testament* contains passages that could be (and in some incidents have been) construed as divine endorsements of wife-beating, racial warfare, slavery, the stoning to death of rebellious children and other behaviors that are outrageous by today's standards. As Shakespeare once wrote, "The devil can cite Scripture for his purpose."

Experts on the sexual danger of spanking have stated:

"It is a disgusting and slavish treatment that they would regard as an insult if they inflicted it on adults. Also consider how shameful, how dangerous to modesty are the effects produced by the pain or fear of the victims. This feeling of shame cripples and unmans the spirit, making it flee from and detest the light of day . . ." (Centillion, A.D. 35-95).

"Often, the avowed disciplinary value of flagellation in schools and colleges was a mere pretense to enable sadists to secure sexual titillation" (George Ryley Scott, a historian, sociologist, anthropologist, *The History of Corporal Punishment, 1986)*.

"These are the realities that most of us remain eager to deny . . . So long as children are beaten by adults, the obsessions with domination and submission, with power and authority, with shame and humiliation, with painful pleasure--all hallmarks of sadomasochism--will remain an enduring consequence of the ordinary violence and coercion done in the name of discipline-- Sadomasochism is not an aberration; it is inherent in corporal punishment . . ." (Philip Greven, professor of history. *Spare the Child*, 1992).

"Spanking on the buttocks can produce definite erotic sensations, including sexual orgasm, in some children. Children sometimes knowingly do things to cause themselves to be spanked. They misbehave on purpose and, by pretending distress while receiving the desired 'punishment,' the adult assumes the child is getting appropriate punishment for the misdeed. The frequency with which this happens is not known, although it may not be altogether rare. In many incidents the spankings are given for the adult's own perverted gratification ('sadism'); or at least there might have been culpable awareness and toleration of the child's sexual reaction by the adult. Only some decades ago, perverts masquerading as a governess or tutors were reportedly anything but rare in some European countries." (J. F. Oliven, pathologist, *Sexual Hygiene and Pathology*, 1965).

"Frequent spankings, too, may have a negative impact on sexual development. Because of the proximity of the sex organs, a child may get sexually aroused when spanked. Or she may so enjoy the making up that follows the punishment that she will seek suffering as a necessary prelude to love. There are many adult couples who seem to need a good fight before a good night." (Dr. Haim G. Ginott, child psychologist, *Between Parent and Child*, 1966).

"Being beaten excites children sexually because it is an intense excitation of the erogenous zones of the skin of the buttocks and of the muscles below the skin. . . "(Otto

Fenickel, M.D. *The Psychoanalytic Theory of Neurosis*, 1945).

"The adult flagellant fantasy, in short, always derives from the infantile one. As with all sexual perversions, we are dealing with a variety of arrested development . . . that puberty and subsequent experience have been unable to dislodge . . . We need to examine its roots in childhood . . . " (Ian Gibson, *The English Vice*, 1979).

The odds that spanking a child will lead to psychosexual aberrations or that spanking leaves a child vulnerable to sexual abuse and incest perpetrators would be difficult to calculate. However, the fact that there is any chance that any of these serious problems might occur is reason enough for parents and childcare workers to do away with the practice of spanking. These risks are completely unnecessary.

Our laws and our cultural values are unambiguous concerning adults who physically attack or verbally threaten other adults. Such behavior is recognized as criminal, and we hold the perpetrators accountable. Why then, when so much is at stake for society, do we accept the excuses of child batterers? Why do we become interested in the needs of children only after they have been terribly victimized, or have become delinquents victimizing others?

The answer is not complicated. We cannot have empathy toward abused children until we can honestly acknowledge the mistreatment from our own childhood experiences and examine the shortcomings of our own parents. To the extent we feel compelled to defend our parents and guard their secrets, we will do the same for others. We will look the other way. By continually insisting that we "turned out okay," we are reassuring ourselves and diverting our attention from deeply hidden unpleasant memories.

This is why, when someone says, "spanking is abuse," many of us react as though a door barricaded since infancy has been smashed open. This barricaded, unconscious door has prevented us from committing the most dangerous, most unpardonable act of disloyalty imaginable, disloyalty to our parents. We are afraid that by opening the door we might fall through into an abyss--abandoned and cut off from any possibility of reconciliation with the parents we love. The fear is irrational. Denial--about what was done to our generation and, now, what we are doing and allowing to be done to the next generation--is the real danger and the real sin.

Reconciliation and healing can only begin with an acknowledgment of the truth. It is futile to hope that lies, evasions and excuses can somehow erase the memory and the pain of past injuries.

There are many excellent workshops and books regarding parenting without spanking. Many community colleges and high school adult school programs offer parenting workshops. All parents who were spanked as children need to be taught about the needs and nurturing of children. A person who was spanked as a child poses a far greater potential for spanking their child than someone who was not spanked.

It is never too late to stop spanking your child. Your child will benefit from discipline via other methods than spanking. Most parents need support and proven alternatives to spanking.

Learn to be a Non-Spanking Parent

The following tips for the purpose of raising children without spanking are easy to implement.

- Identify what you want your child to do—both in the moment and long term. Tell your child what, "to do" rather than what, "not to do." The brain is like a computer. A computer is not programmed with what, "not to do." Likewise, a child needs to be programmed with what, "to do." For example: If your child is touching something you do not want touched, teach your child to 'look' at the item. If it is something that is used, such as a stereo, teach your child some things are for adults only or teach your child which buttons or knobs to turn or push. Children as young as 18 months can learn to push or turn knobs and buttons. However, the focus needs to be on telling your child what 'to do.' If your child is preverbal simply direct (distract) the child away from whatever she or he is doing, instead of yelling, 'No' or hitting.

- Encourage your child to engage in those behaviors you want or approximations of them. Reward small steps.

- Use consequences germane to the transgression instead of spanking.

- Remember to praise immediately for the behavior you want or point it out in a positive way.

- Walk away or leave the room if you are losing your composure or are frustrated and want to scream or hit.

The following books are excellent resources for alternatives to spanking or hitting.

- *Case Against Spanking*, Irwin Hyman
- *Without Spanking or Spoiling*, Elizabeth Crary
- *Instead of Spanking-1001 Alternatives*, Vol. 2, Adah Maurer
- *Discipline Without Shouting or Spanking*, Jerry Wyckoff
- One Hundred One Alternatives to Nagging, Yelling or Spanking, Alvin Price

Good, Appropriate Touch

If this seems as if "no touch" is the "best touch," I want to assure you that there is such a thing as "good touch." Everyone needs touch that soothes and nurtures. Studies on children in orphanages in England during World War II revealed that without touch children become morose (anaclitic depression) and often die despite adequate nutrition and proper hygiene.

The most important guideline in touching your child is respecting your child's likes and dislikes. When your child is nonverbal, you will need to watch for signals, such as: wincing, squirming, holding the breath, or crying to decide if the touch is disliked. Any sign of dislike or discomfort needs to be respected and the activity ceased immediately, without question.

Recently a client asked me if she was accurate in her evaluation of a situation with her 34-month-old son and his father, her husband. In this situation, her husband was holding their son, Mark, above his head and swinging him around. Mark was giggling and squealing. Then Mark said, "No, Daddy." However, Mark continued to giggle and squeal. "No, Daddy," he said, again. Mark's mother said, "Roger, he wants you to stop, he said, 'No.'" "However, he is laughing," Roger replied. "I know he is laughing, but he said, 'NO,'" Mark's mother insisted. "I am listening to his words and he said, 'No.' We need to respect what he says," she continued. Roger then put Mark down. Although Mark stopped laughing and squealing, he did not ask for the activity to continue. Therefore, we can be assured his "No" meant he wanted the activity to cease.

Respecting and honoring your child's preferences, including while playing, is critically important. When you ignore your child's preferences you are in fact, effectively saying, "Your perceptions do not count." Your child will soon learn through lack of respect and disregard to their preferences, that they have no power. When we believe we are powerless with the most trusted people in our lives (our parent[s]), we will cease to exercise power with anyone. Granted, if Roger continued to swing Mark the ill effects might be minimal. However, on a broader scale the outcome could be catastrophic. Children learn their life skills vis-a-vis their parents. If they perceive themselves as powerless with their parents, they will be powerless with other adults, thus, other adults could include a perpetrator who is waiting for just such a child to become their next victim.

As described in the incident with Mark and his father, laughing can be a mixed message. Although the child is laughing, squealing or giggling, when he or she says, "No," "don't" or "stop," we need to respect what the child says. Or at times when the laughter is at a level that causes the child to lose his or her breath, the touching or activity may have crossed the threshold of pleasure to pain. In this instance, stop immediately and redefine the activity. Explain to your child, "I am changing the play to avoid your losing your breath." If your child is verbal and begs you to continue, and you are inclined, do so with modification. Avoid implying you stopped the play because the child was not responding or playing as you wanted. Children want to please, even when it is a play activity. If the child thinks he or she has displeased you, he or she will attempt to hide any discomfort they are experiencing.

Good touch includes: gently rubbing your child's back, arms, hands, fingers, head, cheeks, ears, forehead, feet and toes. Rubbing their legs needs to be modified to avoid the inner thigh, which is a highly erogenous area. Blowing air bubbles (a.k.a. raspberries) on their stomach is every child's delight. Avoid the chest area, a highly erogenous area.

CAUTION: Remember--As the parent or caretaker, you know your motives when you touch a child. "What is wrong with giving my child a pat on the bare buttocks as a show of affection? What is wrong with kissing my baby on the bare buttocks after he or she has had a bath?" you might ask. There is probably nothing wrong, and these actions would not be considered boundary violations. However, what your child is learning via this activity is what is acceptable touch with someone the child trusts. Perpetrators use acceptable, affectionate touch for bonding and desensitizing the child. If the child is accustomed to being patted on the buttocks by the parent, their predisposition to this form of touch would likely leave them vulnerable in allowing anyone whom they trust to do the same. Thus, someone who is a perpetrator can begin the desensitization process seemingly innocently with an increased possibility of the child's compliance. Therefore, if the child does not protest when he or she is patted on the buttocks, the perpetrator accepts this as confirmation the child is accustomed to being patted on the buttocks and may progress to sexual touching. If your child is not accustomed to being patted on the buttocks and you have instructed him or her to protest to this form of touch, the perpetrator may be reluctant to go further.

In addition, with the TELL MOMMY AND DADDY EVERYTHING--NO SECRETS RULE, which is explained in detail later in this chapter, your child will remain more likely to inform you of occurrences involving unwanted or inappropriate touch.

Hugging is the most magnificent form of touching. Hugging can say things like: "I am here for you," "I really understand your feelings," "I am proud of you," "Allow me to comfort you," "I love you," and much more.

There are 14 different types of hugs: The A-frame hug, Ankle hug, Side-to-thigh hug, Back-to-front hug, Bear hug, Cheek hug, Custom-tailored hug, Grabber-squeezer hug,

Group hug, Guess who hug, Heart centered hug, Sandwich hug, Side-to-side hug, Top-of-the-head hug. Each of these basic hug types has many variations. Thus, hugs can account for the majority of the touch you give your child.

Tickling is a very "ticklish" kind of touch. No pun intended for this very serious subject. Many sexual abuse or incest survivors state their abuse started with tickling. However, in many incidents, the child intuitively knew that the tickling was different in nature, but did not know they had a right to protest. Therefore, if you tickle your child, be extremely watchful where you tickle. Avoid highly-erotic areas such as the buttocks, breast area, groin, or inner thigh. These precautions apply equally to boys and girls. Additionally, reinforcing the lesson that your child has the right to protest is advisable if the tickling, for any reason, is uncomfortable. It is imperative you stop any tickling if your child displays any signs of discomfort. Stop! Then say, "I am sorry, I did not mean to hurt you."

Teach Your Child Self-Protection through Body Boundaries

Teaching additional self-protection begins when the child is learning to talk. Self-protection includes verbal instruction, "No one touches your body, your body is yours." "No one (Mommy, Daddy, Grandmother, Grandfather, Uncle, Aunt) can touch your body if you do not like it." Naming exactly whom you mean when you say, "no one" is important. The emphasis of "no one" includes people the child trusts, such as family members, teachers, friends' parents, caretakers, etc.

This lesson can be introduced in stages. Begin by playing the game of identifying their eyes, nose, ears, etc. When your child has learned to identify their eyes, nose, ears, etc., introduce the following specific dialogue. For example: "You are a special, beautiful, perfect [boy/girl]. Where are your eyes?" When the child points to his or her eyes, say, "That is right, your eyes are special. Where is your nose?" When the child points to his or her nose, compliment her by saying, "That is right." Then add, "Your nose is special." Go through this routine until they have identified all body parts and you have emphasized that each body part is "special." This lesson needs to be repeated frequently. It can be done spontaneously when dressing, undressing, and bathing or whenever a quiet moment permits. Remember to include penis, scrotum, testicles, labia and vagina.

The second stage begins when the child has begun using simple sentences. Choose time when both you and your child will have uninterrupted time alone. Repeat, "Your body is private, special, perfect and beautiful. No one has the right to touch you. No one is allowed to touch your body, if you do not like it--your body is yours. No one (Mommy, Daddy, Grandmother, Grandfather, Uncle, Aunt) can touch your body if you do not like it." Just like no one can touch your [name your child's favorite toy that she or he does not share with anyone or no one can touch], no one has the right to touch you if you do not like it."

Teach this part of the lesson through demonstration. Touch the child's thigh, buttocks, waist, arms, etc. Then instruct the child to say, "No touching" or "Stop" in a firm, loud voice. Repeat this lesson until it is well-learned. This is vitally important, because if you leave your child with anyone, including family members who you believe are trustworthy, she has your permission to protest unwanted touch.

Your child might say, "Mommy, you and Daddy touch me." Be glad your child has said this. You now know she or he has understood your message. Calmly reply: "Yes, Mommy and Daddy touch you. We need to help you take care of yourself until you can do it for yourself. If Mommy or Daddy touches you and it is uncomfortable, you can say, 'No touching or Stop.' Mommy or Daddy will stop." Then you need to honor this request without question. Stop whatever you are doing immediately. Apologize, "I am sorry, I did not mean to touch you in a way that you did not like." Then either cease the activity or continue in a different way.

Parents need to instruct and encourage their children to cooperate and follow these instructions; the child needs to be encouraged to stop unwanted touch by anyone at anytime. Yes, we want our children to cooperate; however, they need to know that they can protest when something does not seem right. Allow the child to trust her intuitiveness. When you witness or are told your child has exercised her right to protest touch, reinforce the lesson by complimenting her. "I am glad you said, 'No touching my arm,' when Ms. Smith took a hold of your arm. You did a good job taking care of yourself."

This instruction coupled with your interceding whenever anyone touches your child and she or he protests, portrays a clear message that you will support her on this issue. Thus, she will feel confident to follow through when alone. When she tells you about protesting unwanted or uncomfortable touch, avoid overriding her decision by saying such things as, "I don't think Ms. Smith would hurt you." Your child needs to exercise her perception of what she deems unacceptable or uncomfortable touch. A child will test to see if you will support them. She or he will protest with someone they feel safe with to make sure you will support their decision. If you support their decision, they will be confident to risk protesting with anyone. This testing is part of the learning process. If you override their decision they will become confused or conflicted and doubt their ability to trust their intuitiveness. Remember, what is uncomfortable to her is the key determination in protesting touch.

A mother asked me what she could do for her son, age 37 months. She had taught him to protest anyone's actions he did not like. However, he barely raised his voice in protest when his grandmother touched him in a way he did not like. This mother was dismayed, saying, "He starts preschool in only six weeks." I reassured her that she had done everything correctly in teaching her son to protest. This incident was merely an opportunity for her to reinforce the lesson. I instructed her to remind her son of the incident, "Remember when Grandma took your diaper off and you did not want her to do that? I heard you say something, but I did not know you were upset. Next time you need to say, 'Don't do that,' really loud." I also instructed the mother to have him practice until she was satisfied he understood the volume necessary to alert her that something was wrong.

You might be concerned whether your child will tell you the truth void of exaggeration or distortion. It is unlikely that your child will exaggerate or distort, unless he or she tends to exaggerate or distort in other situations or circumstances. Having worked with more than 100 survivors of sexual abuse and incest, the only distortion I have encountered is the propensity of the survivor to minimize the abuse rather than exaggerate it. Meiselman wrote, "There is no evidence that reports of incest are more likely to be false or grossly distorted than are reports of other kinds of emotionally charged events in a person's case history, especially when the incest report is given so long after the event that there is no immediate motive for fabricating it." If you respect your child's perception in other situations and you have reason to trust him or her then, likewise, you can trust your child's perception in this situation.

Teach Your Child Good Body Image

When teaching your child about his or her body, include penis, testicles, scrotum, labia and vagina. Children have curiosity and questions about these body parts anyway. If you treat such questions and conversations as matter-of-fact, you will eliminate any uneasiness for either you or your child. Girls' genitals are often referred to as, "down there," which begs the question: "What is it, what is the mystery?" Avoid using "made-up" names--use labia, vagina, penis and scrotum as you would for any other body part. Avoid conveying any uneasiness you might have. Emphasize the fact that "Everyone's body is private, special, beautiful, and perfect." The more the child knows about his or her body, the more he or she can take ownership. Ownership and a sense of pride in one's body enhance one's ability to command boundary limitations. There are several excellent books on the facts of life to augment this lesson.

Tell Mommy and Daddy Everything--No Secrets Rule

Teach your child to **TELL YOU EVERYTHING. NO SECRETS. NO SECRETS** from Mommy or Daddy. Secrecy is a necessary component used to control the sexual abuse victim. Perpetrators cannot continue abuse with a child or other closely accessible children unless secrecy prevails.

Abusing children over several generations is common for some perpetrators. Force is rarely used--the child's natural dependence and powerlessness are used against her. The closer the relationship, the less force is necessary and the less likely the perpetrator needs to rely on physical dominance. Mothers, upon learning their child or adult child was sexually abused, often say, "I had no idea, if I had known I would have done something." If the **TELL MOMMY AND DADDY EVERYTHING--NO SECRETS RULE** had been taught, I contend the child would have told someone about the occurrence if the child's rights to ownership of his or her body, preferences and truthtelling techniques had been acknowledged and encouraged. In circumstances such as these, the perpetrator would be less likely to subtly touch the child without the mother being alerted by the protests. This would be especially true if, for example, the father said, "Let's not tell Mommy, this is our special [time or secret]." She might conform to secrecy or silence for a brief period of time; however, the guilt about being silent or keeping the secret from her mother would validate what her intuitiveness was telling her, "Something is wrong." She would eventually tell.

Instruct your child to tell you if anyone says anything such as, "This is a secret," "This is our secret," "Don't tell anyone," "If you tell your Mom or Dad, they'll be mad," etc. Reinforce the concept with your child that she or he is not obligated to keep secrets or be silent. Assure your child that they can tell you anything and everything anyone says or does, and you will listen to him or her. Make it a practice of listening to your child when she or he tells you anything.

Tell Mom my and Daddy Everything--No Secrets Rule in Action

Teaching your child the **TELL MOMMY AND DADDY EVERYTHING--NO SECRETS** rule means parents need to practice telling the child the truth. The **TELL MOMMY AND DADDY EVERYTHING--NO SECRETS** rule means the parents cannot say, "Don't tell Mommy, Daddy, Grandma or Grandpa, we want this to be a surprise." Avoid putting your child in the position of determining which "secrets" need to be kept and which ones can be revealed. Children under age 5 or 6 can become confused in determining which secrets to keep and which to reveal. Therefore, parents can't expect their child to keep any secrets. If something needs to be kept "secret," keep it away from the child's awareness. Yes, it might take more work on your part, but it is worth the effort.

The benefits of the **TELL MOMMY AND DADDY EVERYTHING--NO SECRETS** rule far outweigh any inconveniences. The **TELL MOMMY AND DADDY EVERYTHING--NO SECRETS** rule has other benefits; you are empowering and supporting your child to command dignity and respect. The **TELL MOMMY AND DADDY EVERYTHING--NO SECRETS** rule needs to be honored at all times in the presence of children. When it is necessary to discuss issues that are not appropriate for the child to hear, parents need to wait until they are alone. You need to avoid referring to the issue or using code words. Children quickly learn when parents use code words and wonder "What is the secret?"

Tell Mommy and Daddy Everything--No Secrets Rule Works

A mother relates, "My son at age 10 spent the night at a friend's house. His friend's father fondled my son's penis as he slept. It awakened my son and he pushed his hand away. The fondling stopped and my son went back to sleep. The next day my son told me he did not want to stay overnight with his friend anymore. Questioning revealed the reason."

This incident could have become ongoing abuse. However, because the boy had been taught **"TELL MOMMY AND DADDY EVERYTHING--NO SECRETS"** and "your body is yours" and "no one has the right to touch you in ways you dislike," he reported the incident. The perpetrator, known for his generous volunteering at school, was considered trustworthy and the least likely suspect.

The **TELL MOMMY AND DADDY EVERYTHING--NO SECRETS RULE** and "your body is yours" also worked when John, 3 years old, was abused by two 10-year-old boys. JM was a victim of incest for many years by his father, whom his mother had divorced. John's mother knew this, but she did not suspect JM would abuse another child, especially since he was a family friend. After playing in the backyard, while the two mothers talked inside, John said, "Mommy, JM and that boy held me down and took my pants off and touched my penis." John's mother sought professional intervention immediately. She had taught John the **NO SECRETS** rule and "your body is yours," which she believes empowered her son to tell her what he experienced, possibly preventing another incident.

Another mother relates, "My 12-year-old daughter thwarted her perpetrator, her teacher. He asked her to help him take some equipment to his office. He closed his office door as he walked behind her. She put the things she had carried on his desk and turned to leave. He was in front of her, too close for comfort. He put his hand on her shoulder. He said, 'You are a nice girl and pretty too.' He then reached and stroked her hair. 'We could be good friends,' he said. At this point she knew something was wrong. Her heart pounding, she rushed out the door. She told me when she got home. I contacted the school and the police. Because there were other reports to the police about this man regarding sexual misconduct, they arrested him. Through a plea bargain, he did not go to jail, but he did lose his teaching license and was on probation for five years."

A 26-year-old woman remembers a weekend trip with her father when she was 6 years old. "As an adult, I know my father attempted to seduce me sexually. At the time I felt confused and angry. I knew he wanted me to do something, but I did not know what it was. It just did not feel right. He put a peeled banana in his mouth and sucked on it--then he wanted me to suck on it. I refused! Then he pulled me to sit on his lap. I was angry. I screamed at him and wrenched away from his hold. The next day when my mother and brother came I was still very angry. My mother questioned me about why I was so angry. I told her what he did. She considered it an attempt to abuse me sexually. At the time she was contemplating a divorce due to my father's abuse of alcohol. She says this incident hastened her decision. I know if I did not know about self-protection, I would not have known what to do. Although I did not know what he wanted, I knew something was wrong. Telling my mother gave her information she used to protect me."

Without the Tell Mommy and Daddy Everything--No Secrets Rule

Studies reveal that teaching a child to say "NO" has little impact because it is rare a child will affect more than weak resistance against a known perpetrator. Furthermore, the perpetrator will usually ignore a simple "NO." The perpetrator uses subtle or blatant threats, intimidating the child into compliance and silence.

With family members, although the child does not like this strange affection, she is confused because she loves the perpetrator and does not believe they would do anything wrong. Without the awareness that "my body is mine, and no one, not even Mommy or Daddy, has the right to touch me in ways I don't like," conflict and confusion follow. In the confused loyalty between victim and perpetrator, the child protects the abuser by holding the secret. The child then carries the shame of her perpetrator, because the child believes he or she has "cooperated." The child places inappropriate blame on himself or herself.

Although when the child says, "NO," it has little impact, coupled with another parental instruction **TELL MOMMY AND DADDY EVERYTHING--NO SECRETS**, the child feels the duality. This duality compels the child to tell, thus promoting proper intervention.

Appropriate Suspicion

The frightening truth about sexual abuse and incest perpetrators is that within their pathology they do not hold beliefs reflecting society's moral and ethical values. Because of a child's innocence and trust of the abuser, usually pressure or violence is not required. Thus, the sexual abuse or incest perpetrator can unequivocally state, "Never ever. I could never harm a child or anyone. It's not in my heart. It's not who I am."

Sexual abuse and incest perpetrators generally pass lie detector tests. They feel no inner conflict with what they have done. Their moral and ethical values do not reflect the standards on which the test is based. If you have the slightest cause for concern, trust your intuition and seek professional intervention. Trusting and acting on our intuition or sixth sense is paramount to protecting children from perpetrators, no matter whether they are family members, family friends, doctors, dentists, teachers, etc.

When intuitiveness or a sixth sense has been activated in detecting danger, it can be identified by a change in one's physiology. The most common changes are:

* Heart rate increase.
* A sense one's blood is draining out or feeling cold.
* Sweaty palms.
* Goose bumps.
* Nervousness/anxiousness.
* Butterflies in stomach.
* Feeling sick to the stomach.
* A general sense of uneasiness.

In addition your intuition is in operation when you experience:

* Confusion regarding a person's actions.
* Nagging/persistent thoughts or feelings.
* Hesitation.
* General suspicion.

* Apprehension.
* Fear.
* Doubt.
* A hunch.
* Curiosity regarding a person's actions or statements.
* Questions regarding a person's proclamation that is not substantiated by their actions.

Although the intuition process can protect us from danger, it is only as effective as we heed the warning signals. Understandably, no one wants to believe his or her spouse or anyone whom they trust would harm, much less sexually abuse, their child. However, the reality is--the overwhelming majority of children are sexually abused by their fathers, followed statistically in this abuse by uncles or grandfathers. Stepfathers who abuse their stepchildren constitute the third largest percentage of sexual abuse perpetrators.

If you fail to heed your intuitive signals you will then accept its diabolic competitor, the denial process. Denial protects us from what we do not want to know. Denial eliminates the discomfort of accepting the horrific reality we do not want to acknowledge. As with intuition, denial prompts recognizable signals. If you detect these signals within yourself, you can stop and ask yourself an empowering and powerful question: "What am I stopping myself from knowing?"

Signals of denial include:

*Accepting the person's explanation about their behavior in lieu of your intuition.

* Minimizing what you know to be true.
* Justifying someone's behavior.
* Rationalizing someone's behavior.
* Refusal to believe what you suspect to be true.
* Excuse-making.

One mother recalled her 4-year-old daughter Jane's behavior when she came home after running errands with her father. He had bought her a stuffed rabbit. This mother was shocked when her daughter threw the rabbit on the floor, stating, "I don't want that rabbit." This behavior was uncharacteristic; she loved stuffed animals. "What is wrong?" this mother asked. Upon questioning, she discovered her daughter was upset because she was asked by her father to "do something" in order to be rewarded with a toy. This mother questioned her daughter regarding what "doing something" meant. [She refused to accept her daughter's statement as merely a moody child's statement.] Her daughter could not explain what she meant. Fortunately, for Jane, her mother did not negate this seemingly innocuous incident and conversation. She investigated further, even though her husband's casual explanation of their daughter's refusal of the stuffed toy was that Jane was "just moody" that morning. [She did not accept her husband's explanation about the situation in lieu of her intuition.] She kept her intuitive antenna alert for several weeks. Ultimately, she discovered to her shock and horror her husband was sexually touching and fondling their daughter.

A client, who is a sexual abuse survivor reported seeing her father (her perpetrator) kiss her 1-year-old niece on the pubic area after she took her bath. "I got sick to the stomach," my client stated. "Is this sexual abuse?" she asked. "I don't know if I am overreacting [refusal to believe her intuitive signal--feeling sick to the stomach-- was valid]." I asked her, "Given what you know about your father, what do you think is going on?" "He probably doesn't know what he is doing [excuse-making]. He probably thinks he is just being affectionate [justification]. If I say anything, they will say I am overreacting and causing trouble [rationalizing]. I have always been called the troublemaker in the family. I don't want to be the troublemaker [justification]."

Many children report sexual abuse, although it may not be stated as such. Unfortunately, the parent frequently disregards the statement. Recently, a 39-year-old client who sought therapy because of a severe panic attack remembered being fondled by a "nice man" who was a friend of the family. She recalled, "He only fondled my breast briefly [minimizing]." When she told her mother of the incident, her mother said, "He probably didn't mean to touch you [excuse-making]."

After reading the first edition of Protect Your Child from Sexual Abuse Perpetrators, a mother called to clarify her intuitive reaction to the game her husband played with their 3-year-old son. Her husband took all of his clothes off, except his under shorts. He taught his son to play a game of "tickle." In this "game" the son was to tickle his father's nipples while sitting in a straddled position over his father's mostly nude body. "Is this sexual abuse?" She asked. "What is your intuition telling you?" I asked. "I don't know for sure. I feel nauseous when I see it [refusal to believe what her intuition is telling her]," she replied. "Besides, what can I do, [justification] it is only my word against his [rationalization]? What if he doesn't mean any harm [excuse-making]? Maybe he doesn't know it will harm our son [excuse-making]." Fortunately, our conversation convinced her that she needed to take action to protect her son. She called Child Protective Services. The outcome was far better than she imagined. Her husband had been sexually abused as a child, which he had never told her. With therapy they regained a stable, healthy family life.

If you witness touch that seems inappropriate for your child, but feel a sense of guilt in knowledge that your perception may be inaccurate [refusal to accept one's perception], trust yourself.

Last but not least, no matter how confident you are in your ability to detect a perpetrator, you need to take a final precaution. Periodically check on your child when anyone is alone with him or her. If your spouse is dressing, bathing or putting your child to bed, casually enter the room. Note whether your spouse acts surprised, caught off guard or generally uneasy that you entered the room unannounced. Follow this procedure of unannounced visits, regardless of who is tending to your child at any given time. Be on alert for reactions of surprise, being caught off guard or general uneasiness in response to your presence. Many daycare facilities have video cameras for parents to check their child's activities via the Internet. However, never assume that your child is safe from perpetrators, even in a monitored environment.

If you doubt your ability to clearly decide if there has been abuse or abuse might occur, contact a psychotherapist who specializes in sexual abuse recovery; this could be the key to uncovering and stopping the abuse.

Sexual abuse and incest perpetrators usually state they love children (even if perverse and insidious) and do not perceive their behavior as harmful to the child. Indeed, perpetrators who acknowledge their sexually abusive behavior often make statements such as, "I love children. If I had known it was hurting them, I would have never done it. I never intended to hurt anyone." While this may be true, it does not change the fact the harm was done, nor does it eliminate their responsibility for their actions.

Some perpetrators perceive the child as merely an object of their obsession. One man, who abused 40 children, thought that everyone understood his perception of his victims as objects. He expressed astonishment when a woman asked him how he could do those things to babies. While in therapy, he asked, "Didn't she know those children were objects to me?" Another male perpetrator said he never thought that the children might have feelings about the sexual abuse.

Jane F. Giligun and Teresa M. Connor conducted a study of 14 male sexual abuse perpetrators ranging in age from 21 to 54. All these men believed that they had deep and loving relationships with their victims. However, all perpetrators are placing their desires ahead of the rights of their victims.   As one man said, "We had a relationship. Right or wrong, it was a relationship."

Most perpetrators go to great lengths to present themselves as exemplary people. For example: the school teacher, who frequently stays after school to help a child with academic difficulties; a parent who takes time away from work to accompany the students on field trips; the Little League coach who fosters a relationship with a fatherless child.

I am not suggesting that everyone who does these things is a sexual abuse or incest perpetrator.   However, insidiously, perpetrators demonstrate the right, moral and exemplary behavior to develop credibility and establish proof of their love of children; these actions thus thwart any suspicion of wrongdoing, thus allowing access to lure the innocent, trusting child.

However, in looking closely at the total picture of this exemplary behavior, we can detect discrepancies. The sexual abuse or incest perpetrator's behavior in the dynamic has shrewdness beneath its exterior.   The perpetrator works to create "a public image of goodness." They are extraordinarily helpful, willing, accommodating, solicitous, and profess their love of children frequently (this is especially true of their victim or sexual abuse target). They are anxious about being accepted as a good, moral and ethical person. They frequently volunteer to work with children on projects or in situations where a child needs one-on-one attention.   They solicit comments for their exemplary   performance,   thus   directing   people's perceptions. Non-perpetrators who help children do so because they genuinely want to help children. Because there is no ulterior motive (i.e. building their image of public goodness) they generally do not solicit comments regarding their good deeds and humbly accept a "thank you," when it is offered.

In addition, if we look closely, we will notice that the sexual abuse or incest perpetrator frequently fosters a close bond with a child and does so more at his own insistence and behest than that of the child's. Thus, "the perpetrator is using the child and treating her in a way that is not wanted or not appropriate by a person with whom a different relationship is required. If the experience has meaning for another person, in lieu of a nurturing purpose for the benefit of the child, it is abuse."

In a study of 20 adult sexual abuse perpetrators conducted by Jon Conte, Steven Wolf and Tim Smith; two of the key questions asked were:

1. "Was there something about the child's behavior which attracted you to the child?" The responses included:

   - "The warm and friendly child or the vulnerable child... Friendly, showed me their panties."
   - "The way the child would look at me, trustingly."
   - "The child who was teasing me, smiling at me, asking me to do favors."
   - "Someone who had been a victim before, quiet, withdrawn, compliant. Someone, who had not been a victim would be more non-accepting of the sexual language or stepping over the boundaries of

modesty… Quieter, easier to manipulate, less likely to object or put up a fight…goes along with things."

2. "After you had identified a potential victim, what did you do to engage the child into sexual contact?" The responses included:

- "I didn't say anything. It was at night, and she was in bed asleep."
- "'Talking, spending time with them, being around them at bedtime, being around them in my underwear, sitting down on the bed with them… Constantly evaluating the child's reaction… A lot of touching, hugging, kissing, snuggling."
- "Playing, talking, giving special attention, trying to get the child to initiate contact with me… Get the child to feel safe to talk with me… From here I would initiate different kinds of contact, such as touching the child's back, head… Testing the child to see how much she would take before she would pull away."
- "Isolate them from any other people. Once alone, I would make a game of it (e.g., red light, green light with touching up their leg until they said stop). Making it fun."
- "Most of the time I would start by giving them a rub down. When I got them aroused, I would take the chance and place my hand on their penis to masturbate them. If they would not object, I would take this to mean it was okay… I would isolate them. I might spend the night with them… Physical

isolation, closeness, contact are more important than verbal seduction."

Ironically, the mother of a 10-year-old boy wondered if there was an ulterior motive by the father of her son's classmate, Greg. In addition to frequent volunteering, he took his son Greg and classmates to museums and plays on Broadway. "Stop being so suspicious," she told herself. "He is wealthy, owns a business, can set his own hours; therefore, he could volunteer at school. Isn't that what we want from fathers--more involvement with their children?" Four years after the two boys met and befriended each other, this father sexually abused his son's classmate, Jeff, while the two boys slept in Greg's room.

We cannot ignore the sophistication of sexual abuse or incest perpetrators' efforts to desensitize the child through the gradual development of a relationship with the child and progressing from non-sexual touch (e.g., touching a leg or back) to sexual touch.

A client who has many classic aftereffects of sexual abuse revealed that her perpetrator grabbed her breast and squeezed it as he helped her on with her coat when she was 9 years old. This incident was the only incident she recalls. She did not tell anyone. "To what end?" she asked herself. "He was considered a 'nice' gentleman, who helped ladies on with their coat. Who would believe me? Besides, it was only once and how much harm could it cause? I felt betrayed and sick to my stomach at the time," she recalled. Now she knows how much harm an isolated incident such as this can cause and realizes the source of the classic aftereffects she has suffered with for the past 26 years.

For the child who has not been taught the techniques of self-protection, one of the consequences of this relationship building and desensitization process is one of self-blame; by the time the child realizes that abuse is taking place, the child may believe she has given consent to the abuse. She thinks because she did not say "no" when he rubbed the back of her head, she is to blame.

However, as the incidents revealed demonstrate, a child taught the techniques of self-protection will know she can protest whenever the touch moves from that of acceptable to unacceptable touch. However, more importantly, if she is abused, she will know what to do.

It is absolutely critical that all concepts of self-protection (good body image, body boundaries, acceptable or un-acceptable touch based on the perception of the child, and Tell Mommy and Daddy Everything--No Secrets Rule) are taught, reinforced and supported.

We need to accept the reality that no one can be considered exempt from being a perpetrator, including a child's father or mother. As a parent, be appropriately suspicious. Check in the bathroom when anyone is bathing your child or dressing/undressing him or her. If the person seems uncomfortable, behaves as if he is covering up something or acts as if they were caught when you walk in, check again under the same circumstances. If the same reaction occurs, check the possibility that your child might be the victim of sexual abuse. Ask your child, "Did [name suspect] touch you in ways you do not like?" If your child shows signs of distress after spending time alone with anyone, including your partner, ask what is bothering her.

If your partner or anyone instructs your child to tickle, touch or rub him or her in erotic areas of the body, this is an activity that is sexual for the receiver and inappropriate for the child. "It is abuse because it does not take into consideration the needs or wishes of the child; rather, it meets the needs of the other person at the child's expense. If the experience has sexual (erotic) meaning for another person, in lieu of a nurturing purpose for the benefit of the child, it is abuse. If it is unwanted or inappropriate for her age or the relationship, it is abuse."

Several women, who have many classic aftereffects of sexual abuse, have reported that their fathers frequently cuddled with them in bed while wearing only shorts or pajamas. Some described their father as holding them in a spoon position. Several women reported feeling their father's penis against their legs or back. One woman reported her father putting his leg over her, thus, she felt trapped. This cuddling may seem harmless to an adult. After all, we want fathers to be affectionate and give their children attention. However, for the child it is a different experience. In each instance, the woman remembered she felt she was doing something she did not want to do, yet she did not believe she could refuse.

"If a child is forced into an experience that is sexual in content or overtones [for the other] that is abuse. As long as the child is induced into sexual activity with someone who is in a position of greater power, whether that power is derived through the perpetrator's age, size, status, or relationship, the act is abusive. A child who cannot refuse, or who believes she cannot refuse, is a child who has been violated."

How, you might ask, would the child experience sexual overtones by cuddling with her father in bed? The fact that the experience can be construed as sexual is quite understandable. At birth, children are complete, neurological sexual beings who can experience erotic sensation although they are sexually immature and without an active sex drive. Thus, the child senses the sexual overtones of the parent; therefore, it is perceived as sexual, thus unwanted and inappropriate for the child and the relationship.

If the child understood that he or she had the right to protest when the touch did not feel comfortable, he or she would feel more confident in protesting or moving away from that form of touch or cuddling. This act of self-protection empowers her against feeling powerless, defenseless or trapped. Thus, it mitigates the severity of the shame, guilt or confusion. She has refused. Lest we forget, "Incest is both sexual abuse and an abuse of power . . . A child who cannot refuse, or who believes she cannot refuse, is a child who has been violated."

Furthermore, by initiating and practicing the **TELL MOMMY AND DADDY EVERYTHING--NO SECRETS RULE** your child will be more likely to tell you if an activity is uncomfortable. She may not know what you need to know or how to tell you. Nevertheless, your child will be more inclined to tell you something. As with the 26-year-old woman who remembered her father's violation of her at age 6, she did not know what her father wanted, only that it did not feel right. She protested and wrenched away from him. The next day, she did not know what to tell her mother. However, her anger was apparent, thus giving her mother a clue that something was wrong. Fortunately for her, her mother did not accept her anger as merely "a child's bad temper." Her mother investigated, asking questions that would form a clear understanding of the actions that prompted her daughter's anger.

Therefore, it is imperative that you trust your child's perception of her experience. When she tells you about her experiences, no matter what they are, ask simple questions that require a "Yes" or "No" answer until you fully understand what she is telling you. Avoid making assumptions or determining the importance of what your child tells you about anything until you have asked several questions and have clarified the answers.

The exchange between Cindy and her mother is an excellent example of how to uncover what your child is telling you. Initially, Cindy's mother did not give an answer to Cindy's question, "Mommy, can I take my panties off outside?" She investigated to understand what prompted Cindy to ask such a question. Cindy's mother could have simply said, "No, you cannot take your panties off outside." The discussion would have ended and Cindy would probably heed this prohibition. However, she would remain vulnerable to Billy's potential abuse. The possibility Billy would approach her again is very high. Thus, without investigating, Cindy's mother would have unknowingly left Cindy vulnerable to future abuse.

For example, in future instances, Billy might ask Cindy to take her panties off inside; if her friend, Billy's sister, demonstrated taking them off inside, it might seem acceptable. The reason it might seem acceptable is due to the fact that a child's interpretation of an instruction is quite literal to that of an adult. What follows are examples of instruction that could be misinterpreted:

1) Her mother said, "No, you cannot take your panties off outside."
2) Taking panties off inside is customary and the prohibition was for taking one's panties off outside.

Furthermore, although Billy is only 13, the urge to satisfy a compulsion is overwhelming; he would approach Cindy repeatedly until he was stopped or until Cindy was no longer accessible to him. If access to Cindy was denied, he would seek out other victims. He had more immediate access to his two sisters; however, that did not prevent his urge to satisfy his compulsion by approaching Cindy (another child).

Understanding a perpetrator's need to satisfy a compulsion is critical. No matter the age of the perpetrator, or how long he has been a perpetrator, his behavior is directed by an uncontrollable compulsion. He might control himself for periods or under certain circumstances, but he cannot control himself forever. Fear of discovery may hinder his abusive actions or prompt him to control his behavior. He may even want credit for his restraint. Nevertheless, when the pressure builds, and it will build, he will sexually abuse someone again.

We Are Responsible

"Those who ignore the past are condemned to repeat it."

--Sartre

"We are not only responsible for what we do, but also, for that what we don't do."

--Voltaire

"The worst way you can choose is to choose no way at all."

--Friedrich II

"Every choice we make, every thought and feeling we have, is an act of power that has biological, environmental, social, personal and global consequences."

--Caroline Myss

Chapter Six

Signs of Sexual Abuse of Children

The following signs off sexual abuse in children have been thoroughly researched and substantiated. They will help you determine if you child has experienced sexual abuse. Further, any change in your child's behavior can be considered a sign that something is troubling him or her.

Preschool Children:
- Have a sudden fear of specific things, people, places (bathroom or the room where the abuse took place), etc.
- Act out inappropriate sexual activity or display unusual interest in sexual matters.
- Have temper tantrums, especially coinciding with visits to places or interaction with certain people.
- Display violent behavior such as kicking, hitting, biting- -survivors feel extreme frustration and anger.

- Have mood swings, hitting, withdrawal (abused children often feel alone and helpless and withdraw into a shell), culminating into depression.
- Have difficulties with bed wetting or soiling.
- Experience nightmares (monsters, being chased or bogey men), fear of going to bed, or sleepwalking.
- Display physical symptoms of sexual abuse such as pain, itching, vaginal bleeding (bloodstains in panties or pajamas), discharge, redness in genital area, or bladder or kidney infections.
- Have difficulty walking or sitting.
- Experience stomach and digestive problems.
- Complain of flu-like symptoms or not feeling well.
- Display listlessness (robot-like, sitting quietly and unemotionally until someone or something prompts the child to "act").
- Induce self-inflicted pain (head banging, hair pulling, nail biting, body cutting or carving, frequent accidents that cause bodily damage).
- Display regressive behavior: baby talk, sudden clinging behavior.
- Display sudden unexplained aggressiveness or rebellion.
- Insert objects into genitals/rectum - act out sexual behavior on dolls or toys.

Elementary School-Age Children

Elementary school-age children will display all the above and:
- Complain about aches and pains, headaches and other psychosomatic ailments.

- Have unusual knowledge and interest in sex beyond developmental level.
- Display adult or sexualized behavior, (walking seductively, flirting, acting and talking like an adult).
- Have a sudden drop in grades, difficulty concentrating.

Teenagers

Teenagers will display all the above and:
- Have serious depression.
- Have inability to trust others.
- Act out self-destructive behaviors: alcohol and/or drug use, eating disorders.
- Bathe excessively.
- Become secretive.
- Develop strategies for protection such as: layering, wearing baggy or safety-pinning clothes or sleeping on the floor in the closet, under the bed or blocking their door.
- Act out pseudo maturity.
- Acquire sexually transmitted diseases.
- Have a dramatic increase in the frequency of masturbation or masturbation to the point of injury.
- Act out promiscuously.
- Experience serious confusion regarding sexual identity.
- Have an aversion toward opposite sex.
- Have sexual interest in younger children.

Because children often believe a perpetrator's threats or feel shame and guilt, they fail to report episodes of abuse. Parents need to be vigilant for signs and symptoms. Do not accept simple, reasonable explanations on these issues.

The presence of these signs suggests that there is something troubling your child, even if it is not sexual abuse. In any case, you need to determine the causes of the behavioral change. Any change in behavior that does not fit normal stages of development is cause for concern and needs to be investigated and resolved.

Furthermore, be wary if anyone insists she or he needs complete privacy to get to know or bond with your child. Your child can get to know and bond with anyone in your presence. DO NOT ALLOW such contact with your child until your child is verbal and has shown self-empowerment and assertiveness sufficient to thwart any possible abusive behavior.

There are, of course, instances when you will need to entrust your child with others, such as: a pediatrician, child care facility or private child care worker. The following tips on choosing the right pediatrician, child care facility or private care worker will assist you in making this difficult decision.

Chapter Seven

When You Need to Entrust Your Child to the Care of Others

Tips On Visiting The Pediatrician

Selecting the right pediatrician for your child is important. Choose a pediatrician suited for your child's needs. Some basic criteria are as follows:

-Does he or she seem calm and patient or hurried and impatient--taking little time to connect with your child?

-Does he or she take time to get acquainted (reacquainted) with your child each visit?

-Does he or she talk to your child explaining each step before it is initiated?

-Is she or he gentle with and verbally soothes your child if your child cries?

-Does he or she poke and probe unnecessarily?

-Is she or he genuinely interested in your child's emotional and physical development?

Before your child is examined make sure the pediatrician explains each step to your child before it is initiated. Simply state, "Please explain what you need to do before you do it."

When your child learns about protesting when someone touches him or her in ways she or he does not like, you will need to explain before each visit what the doctor or nurses might do and why it is important he or she touches in that way. For example, "The doctor will need to touch your leg to check the lump." If your child asks if it will hurt, and they usually ask, be truthful. "Yes, it might hurt for a while." Avoid going into detail about what it will feel like. If your child wants to opt out, you need to firmly, but lovingly state, "You need to allow the doctor to help you and if it hurts, it will only hurt for a short time." Of course, if surgery is planned the child needs to know it will hurt for some time. Answer all your child's questions clearing and matter-of-fact. Avoid expressing or showing your discomfort or worries.

DO NOT ever allow your child, under age thirteen, to be with a doctor or nurse without your being in the room. At age thirteen or older he or she might be uncomfortable having mom or dad in the room. At this age and because you have taught him or her all the self-protection skills, your child will be safe and will tell you if there are any improprieties. Discuss this with your child prior to the appointment. As you have before with other difficult discussions, be matter-of-fact. "Would you like to go into the examining room alone when you see Dr. Smith next week?" Give your child time to think about this and ask again the day before the appointment. If your child opts to have you in the room, pay close attention as the exam progresses. If you detect any hesitation at answering questions or other signals your child is uncomfortable, ask if he or she would like you to leave the room. If your child says, "yes," nods, or gives the look you know signals a "yes," discreetly leave the room. Avoid thinking your child no longer needs you. Your child needs you as much as ever, but in different ways.

If your child is hospitalized under age thirteen, if at all possible stay with your child twenty-four hours a day. Parents or other family members can take turns staying. Most hospitals have cots to sleep on. If not, a chair is usually available and you can sleep for short periods. Remember helping your child feel safe during a difficult time is important. You would not leave your child with "strangers" under any other circumstance. With nurses changing shifts every eight hours, your child will be with many strangers. When your child is already anxious and stressed because of illness, leaving him or her with "strangers" compounds this difficult experience.

For chronically ill children, staying twenty-four hours a day might not be possible, if they are hospitalized for long periods. I know one couple who took turns staying with their ten-month-old daughter for two weeks. The parents were exhausted, but stated they would do it again if their child was hospitalized.

Tips for Choosing the Right Child Care Facility

The best advice when looking for the right child care facility is to seek reliable recommendations from friends, family or neighbors who can speak from experience. Lists of child care facilities are also available from county social services and the police department.

– Visit frequently without calling first. If this is not allowed, pursue other facilities.

– Investigate every area of the facility. If any area is off-limits for your investigation, chose another facility.

– Make sure bathrooms do not contain areas where a child can be isolated (two-thirds of all daycare sexual abuse takes place in or near the bathroom).

– Investigate supervision during nap time. Are supervisors available at all times? Do they make periodic checks?

– All employees, including volunteers or teachers' aides, who will be interacting with your child, need to pass criminal checks. Also check at least three references.

– If your child is verbal, ask him or her to tell you about times spent alone with anyone, including family members. The following questions will assist you in approaching this issue with your child.

    * "What toys did you play with?"
    * "What did you eat for lunch?"

* "What did you do after lunch?"
* "Who read the story today?"
* "Where did you go?"
* "Who was there?"
* "What games did you play?"
* "Did you play any new games today?"

Children are frequently introduced to sexual activity by playing a game. Make periodic checks for signs of abuse, particularly if your child is non-verbal.

Whether you decide on in-home childcare or out-of-home care the following questions will help you make a choice.

In addition to these interview questions, you might have some criteria that may eliminate a candidate before a formal interview is conducted; these criteria include such things as: own transportation, number of hours, days available, speaking your child's language, non-smoker or non-drinker.

Chapter Eight

Interview Questions for Childcare Workers at Home

1. What are your memories from childhood? Tell the happiest memory. Tell the saddest memory. Tell the worst memory. Tell your favorite memory. The candidate's answers to these questions will give a basic profile of their self-esteem and willingness to reveal themselves.

2. How many siblings do you have? Age and gender? Are you close? Why or Why not?

3. Describe your relationship with your parents.

4. If you could change anything about your childhood, what would it be?

5. How did your parents discipline you? What is your opinion on using physical punishment as discipline? (Although you might use physical punishment as discipline, do not allow anyone else to hit your child for any reason. It is my deepest hope that if you currently use physical punishment as a form of discipline, that the section on physical punishment will prompt your decision

to become a non-spanking parent. If the person says they believe in physical punishment, eliminate them as a candidate.)

6. Do you smoke or use alcohol? (Even though you may smoke or drink, do not allow anyone who smokes or drinks to care for your child. If they are preoccupied with smoking or drinking, your child could remain unattended for periods of time. One mother said she asked a prospective caretaker if she smoked. The woman said, "No." However, the mother could smell smoke on her clothes. She contended that if the woman didn't smoke, but lived with a smoker, she would have revealed that.)

7. Give me an example of the corrective action you would take with my child if (use a circumstance as an example). If you are not satisfied with their method of corrective action, or after explaining your preference and they seem to be unable to conform to your request, eliminate them.

8. I have certain rules for my child. Are you willing to go by those rules too? (If the person needs to know your rules prior to saying "yes," eliminate them as a candidate.)

9. Explain the "TELL MOMMY and DADDY EVERYTHING--NO SECRETS RULE." Ask if they are willing to comply with that rule. (i.e., they are never to say to your child, "This is our secret." "Don't tell your mother or father.") Explain you will be asking your child to tell you what happened in your absence.

Allow your child to meet each candidate. If your child seems comfortable with any of the candidates, choose those candidates for an extensive interview. Using the above questions narrow the candidates to three. For the second interview, allow your child, regardless of your child's age, to interact with each of the three potential candidates. Note any apprehension or distress with your child or the candidate during this phase of the interview.

A mother detailed the second interview with this story:
"I interviewed the three candidates with my son. He was 15 months old. I explained to him that we were talking to these ladies to decide which one would come to play with him while Mommy went to the store, etc. He seemed comfortable with all three initially. Without my asking or suggesting, he climbed onto each one's lap. He sat on one woman's lap for a few seconds. He got off and came over to me and climbed onto my lap. To me, this was a sign that although she seemed like a nice person, he did not feel safe with her. He sat on another woman's lap and then climbed down and went off to play elsewhere. He sat on the third woman's lap for a few minutes. Then, he climbed down and took her by the finger and led her to his toys. He asked her to play with him. I hired her. She has been his caretaker for the past two years."

Children naturally have an acute sixth sense with people. If you have allowed your child to honor their sense of self (i.e., respecting their sacred body boundaries, likes and dislikes regarding touch, etc.) their intuitive sixth sense will not be "clouded" as many adults' have been. Therefore, you can trust that your child will pick the person whose personality will best fit your child. You have already determined the candidates who are acceptable regarding the factual aspect of caring for your child; your child will choose which person's personality fits best.

If your child is less than a year old, you can still trust their intuitive ability. One woman explains her experience.

"My daughter did not like being held by anyone other than me or her father. I was very concerned because I needed to have a caretaker when she was three months old. I needed to go back to work. I thought it would be a nightmare either finding someone she would like or going through her crying every time I left. During the initial interview I asked each person to talk to my daughter while I held her. When I invited three women for the second interview, I asked each woman to talk to her again. I suggested to each woman to invite her to come to her. I had decided that the woman who my daughter went to would be the caretaker and that if she did not go to anyone I would need to start the interview process again. Luckily, my daughter went to two of the three women. She seemed the most comfortable with one woman in particular. The choice turned out to be ideal. She did not cry once when I left. From that experience, I am a firm believer in allowing the child to choose the caretaker. I must say, I was embarrassed because before that my daughter had cried when she was held by my dearest friend."

Many teens are excellent child caretakers. If you are hiring a teenage caretaker, determination of the best candidate based on recommendations is the best approach. If you follow the suggested questions for an adult caretaker, you will undoubtedly find a highly-qualified teen child caretaker.

When your child begins to play with children in your absence or when he or she attends school; you can alert them to the danger of strangers without frightening them. Just as you teach your child to look both ways when crossing the street, you need to alert them to the dangers of the real world. Telling a child about the danger of cars does not create a fear of cars--it provides them the knowledge to possibly prevent serious injury. Simply explain in a matter-of-fact tone that some people harm children. The exact details of how they harm children are not necessary. Teaching your child the survival skills in the following section will make him or her virtually tamper-proof.

Chapter Nine

Survival Skills for Independence

1. Instruct your child to tell you, your spouse or the person in charge before going anywhere, including with anyone he or she knows. This includes where he or she is going, who is going and exactly when he or she will be back.

2. Have a buddy system when your child goes out or plays outside.

3. Do not allow your child to accept gifts of any kind, except pre-approved gifts (birthday, holidays, etc.). Tell your child to seek your approval if someone wants to give them something.

4. Instruct your child to tell you or your spouse if anyone attempts to photograph them.

5.   Instruct your child to NEVER OPEN THE DOOR to anyone in your absence.

6.   Show your child how to find a cashier, security guard or manager in public places in case of separation from you.

7.   Teach your child their phone number and address, as well as proper and timely use of this information.

8.   Teach your child how to dial 911. Many children, as young as three years old, have saved a life because they knew how and when to use 911. Teaching this skill is for everyone's safety.

9.   Teach your child to challenge authority figures, including police officers with badges--"I need to tell my mother or father before I can let you in." Legitimate officials will be cooperative.

10.   Before your child enters kindergarten talk about pornography. Simply explain what pornography is: Pictures showing women's and men's private parts (penis, labia, vagina, and breasts). (Remember: You taught your child their body is beautiful, perfect and private.) Reinforce this lesson by stating: "Everyone's body is beautiful, perfect and private. We do not need to look at pictures of other people's bodies. Their bodies are private. Everyone's body is the same. Male (men or boys) bodies are the same; female (women or girls) bodies are the same. Some people think looking at other people's bodies is okay. Looking at pictures of other

people's bodies is taking their privacy away. Looking at pictures of other people's bodies is the same as anyone opening the bathroom door without knocking when someone is in the bathroom. It is taking their privacy away. We do not want to take other people's privacy away, because we do not want other people to take our privacy away."

11.   Before your child enters kindergarten talk to him regarding the use and danger of drugs and alcohol. Children innocently take offerings from other children, assuming other children, regardless of his or her age, would not do anything to harm them, such as giving them pills or alcohol. The use of alcohol or drugs can leave your child vulnerable to sexual abuse by an older child or adult. Under-age drinking is America's biggest illegal drug problem. A free copy of "What Should I Tell My Child About Drinking?" can be obtained from the National Council on Alcoholism and Drug Dependence (NCADD).

NCADD has the most comprehensive library of materials regarding drug and alcohol prevention. They can be reached at 212-206-6770 ext. 18, or write to: NCAAD at 12 West 21 Street, New York, NY 10010.

Other resources include:

  * National Clearinghouse for Alcohol and Drug Information--800-729-6686
  * Illinois Drug Education Alliance, 85 Bailey Rd, Naperville, IL, 60605, 708-420-1766

* Coalition for the Prevention of Alcohol Problems, 1875 Connecticut Ave NW, Suite 300, Washington, D.C., 20009-5728, 202-332-9110, ext. 343.

Because Survival Skill for Independence Number 10 is a highly controversial issue, I will present additional information.

The U.S. Supreme Court has engaged for decades in a Sisyphean struggle to craft a definition of obscenity to which the lower courts can apply with some fairness and consistency. This struggle led former Justice Potter Stewart to make the now famous statement: "I shall not today attempt further to define [obscenity]; and perhaps I could never succeed in intelligibly doing so. But I know it when I see it."

Women who took a bold stance and developed a detailed definition of obscenity were labeled censorious and anti-sex Victorians. Pornography, they state is "the sexually explicit subordination of women through pictures and/or words." Subordination is defined as depicting "women in postures or positions of sexual submission, servility, or display" or "women are presented in scenarios of degradation, humiliations, injury, torture...in a context that makes these conditions sexual."

The National Coalition Against Pornography, Information and Resources for Concerned Citizens, 1995 stated, "There is no such thing as a 'victimless' crime. In every crime there is a seller or seducer, and the person who purchases, or the seduced. That person is the immediate victim, and society is the ultimate victim, for with each seduction the moral fabric of society is diminished."

Donald E. Wildmon of the American Family Association in *The Case Against Pornography* states that pornography:

- Causes and sustains sexual interest.
- Provides fantasy material which is often acted out in real life.
- Dehumanizes and debases women and reduces sex to a product.
- Teaches that pain and humiliations are "fun" for women.
- Causes men to be less inhibited in committing rape.
- Acts as a sex manual for consumers.

Victor Cline, clinical psychologist, who specializes in treating sex offenders, reported that even soft-core pornography without violence has "the potential of having negative effects on many viewers...modeling unhealthy sex-role behavior or giving misinformation about human sexuality." Dr. Cline believes that the four progressive effects of pornography are:

- Desensitization--user views others as objects.
- Acting out--fantasizing likely becomes overt behavior.
- Addiction--the need to view the material leads to a loss of free control over behavior.
- Escalation--leads the person into progressively harder pornography.

The National Council on Sexual Addiction describes sexual addiction as: "The sexual addict is unable to control his or her sexual behavior and lives with constant pain, alienation, and fear of discovery. The addiction progresses until sex becomes more important than family, friends, or work."

Nobody intends to become addicted to pornography. Nevertheless, every addiction and every addict starts with the first step--the first taste, the first glance, the first sip. Each subsequent step is a little easier until the person is hopelessly hooked. As with any substance addiction, most people do not realize they have an addiction until it is too late. They have crossed the invisible line where there is no turning back--and addiction has become a reality.

A study conducted by the Federal Bureau of Investigation in 1988 revealed that 81 percent of violent sexual offenders regularly read or viewed violent pornography. A Michigan State Police study revealed that pornography was viewed just before or during 41 percent of 48,000 sexual crimes committed over 20 years. "Violent pornography is like a how-to manual for rapists and child abusers," the study concluded. Furthermore, an FBI study on serial homicide concluded that the most common interest among serial killers is pornography.

Serial killer Ted Bundy, who is also a physical and sexual abuse survivor, shed light on pornography in his interview with Dr. James Dobson on January 23, 1989. Bundy was born into a "fine, solid Christian home." At age 12 he discovered pornography. Bundy described his fascination this way. "You keep craving something which is harder, harder...until you reach the point where the pornography only goes so far...an indispensable link in the chain of behavior, the chain of events that led to the behavior, to the assaults, to the murders." Bundy expounded, "I've lived in prison for a long time now, and I've met a lot of men who were motivated to commit violence just like me. And without exception, every one of them was deeply involved in pornography."

The National Coalition for the Protection of Children and Families in 1995 published a study conducted by Seymour Feshback at UCLA. In the study, male students were exposed to violent pornography. After the exposure, 51 percent indicated a strong likelihood of raping a woman if assured they would not get caught.

To ensure availability of children and material, pedophiles develop networks in which they "trade, exchange, and traffic" child pornography—violating the rights of children. These networks usually begin on a local level; however, many extend around the world. London, Ontario is the "kiddie-porn capital" of Canada.

Psychiatrist Frederick Wortham who treats severely troubled children, states, "A child's mind is like a bank-- what goes into it comes back ten years later with interest." A survey on rape at a Kansas City high school illustrates Dr. Wortham's premise; 60 percent of the boys thought it was all right to rape a girl if they thought they were going to marry her.

The following two incidents demonstrate how pornography is distorting our children's thinking. A 10-year-old boy raped and sodomized four younger children in an apartment complex. When police asked him where he got such an idea, the boy showed them his mother's pornography. One 16-year-old boy was required to seek counseling for an addiction to dial-a-porn.

Unfortunately, television is the major source of children's exposure to pornography. *NYPD Blue* has been the most controversial television series in the last decade. It has broken every barrier against nudity and profanity. Many people will argue that *NYPD* is broadcast when young children would be in bed. Furthermore, they argue nudity and profanity are common in our society. But the question remains: At what price?

Children have become desensitized to extramarital affairs, illegitimacy, profanity and the demeaning of the family through such shows as *The Simpsons, Roseanne, Married...With Children, Other Mothers* (an after-school special), *L.A. Law*, soap operas and talk shows. Nowhere has deviant behavior become more the norm than on *MTV*.

Although, you may not allow your child to watch these shows, many parents do allow their children to watch these shows. They do not believe these shows distort children's perceptions. Therefore, even if you dissuade your child from viewing programs such as these, your child will be exposed to other children's beliefs. Thus, you need to equip your child with the information they need to protect themselves. On this basis, I recommend Survivor Skill for Independence Number 10.

Teach your child to tell you if anyone shows them pictures or a movie that shows a person's penis, scrotum, labia, buttocks or breasts.

Many children and adolescents who use or abuse alcohol and drugs are sexual abuse or incest and/or physical abuse survivors. Many survivors in therapy have pondered the question, "Why didn't anyone know I was being sexually abused? I can't understand why no one wondered why I was doing drugs or using alcohol at age [10, 11, 12]. Nobody even asked me if I was sexually abused, and I didn't realize that is why I was drugging and drinking. All everybody did, professionals included, was nag at me about doing drugs or drinking. I was in so much pain, the only way I could stay sane was to numb myself with the strongest substance I could find." I have heard many variations on this pondering. Indeed, why didn't anybody suspect there was something very wrong to compel a child, no matter the age, to begin drinking or drugging? Blaming peer pressure is a simplistic reason. The real problem lies deeper. Getting to the root of your child's willingness to use drugs or alcohol is imperative to solve the issue.

Your child requires specific skills to protect himself or herself against those perpetrators who have easy access to children, such as coaches, teachers, scout leaders, clergy, youth group leaders and recreation leaders. Perpetrators in these groups are particularly difficult to spot because they can easily cover their true motivation for fostering a close relationship with a child. The following survival skills will further "abuse proof" your child.

Survival Skills to Deal with Coaches, Teachers, Scout Leaders, Clergy, Youth Group Leaders, etc.

- Trust and honor your child's intuitive reaction to everyone. (If your child is uncomfortable with anyone, avoid forcing him or her to be in contact with that person. Request a different teacher, join a different league, join a different church or supervise closely if a change is not possible.)

- Beware of anyone bearing gifts. Anyone buying a child a gift is promoting a closer relationship than that of child to teacher, child to coach, child to scout leader or child to clergy, etc. Gift giving is not appropriate behavior for a non-parent or non-family member. Norman Watson, a coach convicted of child sexual abuse, stated he took his player-victims to the mall and bought them games, clothes and athletic equipment. He acknowledged astonishment that parents did not object.

- Be wary of flattery. If a coach or gym teacher says he or she is the one person who can help your "gifted" child develop into a super star or spends an unusually large amount of time with your child, "because he or she is such a wonderful kid" be wary. This is often an overture to win your trust and groom your child for seduction.

- Be present at games and practice. Avoid leaving your child at games and practices alone. This leaves your child vulnerable to being targeted as easy prey. Studies show that men predisposed to molesting children prey first on the child who is regularly left unattended. By being present, you give the message you are actively involved in your child's activities.

- Talk and listen to your child. As emphasized before, listen to your child. Discuss with your child what is inappropriate behavior by a coach, teacher, scout leader, etc. (improper touching, showing pornographic material, etc.) Emphasize the fact that your child can tell you if a coach or teacher says, "Don't tell your parents," about anything he or she is doing. If your child's interest or enthusiasm for school or a sport suddenly diminishes, ask what has prompted the change. Talk with your child until you are satisfied the loss of interest or enthusiasm is related to something other than improper behavior by the teacher, coach, scout leader, etc.

- Stay informed. Make sure you know where the team will be staying on a road trip. If a coach, scout leader or recreation leader says that the presence of the parent hinders team development, be wary. Make sure you know what arrangements are made for showering after games and practices. There is usually no reason for children to be nude in the presence of the coach. There is absolutely no reason for the coach to be nude in the presence of the team.

Tragically, there is no foolproof method of preventing perpetrators from abusing a child. They are cunning predators, who have perfected their skills to get what they want. Therefore, you need to heed and investigate any warning signals (described above). Do not stop until your child's behavior indicates that whatever was troubling him or her is resolved.

If your child tells you she or he has been sexually abused (or makes an implication as such) you need to question him or her immediately. One woman said her 10-year-old son blurted out, "Mr. Smith is a faggot." The intensity of his statement, and the fact her son had never used that word before, alerted her to question why he said such a thing. Questioning revealed Mr. Smith touched her son's penis during the night at a sleep over with Mr. Smith's son. Her son pushed Mr. Smith's hand away and went back to sleep.

Chapter Ten

What To Do if Your Child Reports or Alludes to Having Been a Victim of Sexual Abuse

If your child reports abuse or alludes to abuse, the following tips will help you.

1.   Remain calm.   No matter how upset you are, remain calm to avoid further alarming your child. Your reaction and behavior play a key role in your child's healing.

2.   Understand your child does not know how to tell you or what you need to know. Take your child to a place where she or he will feel safe and protected. Encourage your child to talk about what happened. Record details to ensure accuracy for later use when contacting the police or Child Protective Services.

3.   Avoid discounting anything your child says. Children cannot talk about sexual behaviors unless they have seen or experienced them. Thus, if your child tells

you someone has done something sexual avoid assuming she or he is making it up. If it is not sexual abuse, one needs to question where she or he is hearing such information. If a child falsely accuses someone, something is wrong somewhere, somehow. A false accusation is a cry for help. Investigate until you get the information you need to help your child.

4.   If days or weeks have elapsed since the abuse, avoid asking, "Why didn't you tell me before?" Perpetrators are experts at manipulation, often forcing their victim's silence. Regardless of the time at which your child approaches you with this information, affirm you will protect him or her. Children do not need to be directly threatened to fear repercussions from their assailant. Praise your child for telling you. Never express anger toward or punish your child, even if your child has disobeyed your orders by doing something you have warned them about.

5.   Reassure your child and explain she or he has done nothing wrong. Children easily assume guilt and responsibility for the abuse. They blame themselves because they believe they could have been stronger or smarter.

6.   Get medical attention immediately. Sexual abuse needs to be documented if charges will be pressed later.

7.   Contact the police or Child Protective Services immediately. Generally, confronting the perpetrator does not prompt a confession. You need to take an

official and active role in resolving this matter. Your child needs to witness your actions to reconcile this horrible experience.

8.   Talk about the abuse to only those who need to know about it.   Sexually exploited children are extremely sensitive to comments regarding abuse they've suffered.

9.   Avoid venting your anger or other feelings in front of your child. She or he might assume the fault for upsetting you and regret reporting the abuse, or worse-- recant the story to protect you.

10.   Therapy is paramount for all family members. Children are not emotionally equipped to deal with the trauma of sexual abuse or incest.   Everyone needs therapeutic involvement when one member has been sexually violated. Finding a therapist who specializes in sexual abuse or incest recovery is critically important. 1-800-THERAPIST, a Congressional Award-winning nationwide member referral service, providing mental health resources to persons needing information and services, is an excellent resource for finding the right therapist.

Furthermore, because this is a soul injury, further therapy may be required at other periods during the survivor's lifetime. One such time may be when your child develops a long-term relationship. Not all aftereffects from the abuse can be resolved until the person is in a close intimate relationship of some duration. Review details on aftereffects to relating in intimate relationships. I am a firm believer that victims cannot heal all relationship aftereffects until one is in a relationship of some duration. I have worked with many clients who had therapy after the parent was informed or discovered the abuse. Based on the person's report of their therapy, the therapy seemed to reconcile the issues then, only to be a problem later when they had been in an intimate relationship of some duration. The need for therapy at a later point in time does not suggest that the therapist or therapeutic intervention was inadequate. It attests to the reality of the profound, pervasive and extensive nature of the aftereffects of sexual abuse and incest.

Failure by any knowing adult to protect children from physical or sexual abuse is considered a crime. Any adult who knows of the abuse and has custody of a child can be convicted or lose custody of the child if the abuse continues.

Finally, we are all responsible for the protection of children. Each of us needs to consider this commitment by redefining touch based on the recipient's likes and dislikes of affection, family loyalty and the distribution of power. Redefining these issues is a major undertaking. Perpetrators are not monsters with tails and horns, they are people who are often physical or sexual abuse survivors; however, they cannot be allowed to continue the abuse of innocent children.

To remain in denial about this reality is to accept the role of a co-perpetrator. You can protect your children by empowering yourself and taking full responsibility, supporting their self-esteem, supporting their likes and dislikes regarding touch, and teaching techniques of self-protection.

Knowledge is power. Empower your child with the techniques to protect himself or herself.

"We became what we really are only by the radical and deep-seated refusal of that which others have made us."-
Sartre

Bill of Rights for Children

- The right to adequate nutrition and medical care.

- The right to adequate safety and protection.

- The right to affection, love and understanding.

- The right to express feelings without reprisal.

- The right to express ideas and opinions within the context of the freedom of speech act.

- The right to set boundaries with regard to physical touch.

- The right to full opportunity for play and recreation.

- The right to a name and nationality.

- The right to be among the first to receive relief in times of disaster.

- The right to learn to be a useful member of society and to develop individual abilities.

- The right to be brought up in a spirit of universal peace with sister/brotherhood.

- The right to enjoy these rights, regardless of race, color, sex, religion, nationality or social origin.

Chapter Eleven

Steps to Help Stop Sexual Abuse

1.   Report suspected child sexual abuse to Child Protective Services. Whether the suspected perpetrator is a family member, a friend, a neighbor, a coworker, etc., you need to do whatever you can to protect a child. As an informed adult, to do nothing is to be a co-perpetrator.

2.   Demand child sexual abusers (perpetrators) be held accountable. It is never a child's fault that she or he is sexually abused.

3.   Talk about the problem of sexual abuse whenever the opportunity is right. Silence about this crime is a perpetrator's gain. If you were or are being sexually abused, speak the truth about your experience to anyone who will listen. Talk until you gather a community of support, and ask them to speak against this crime.

4.   Encourage anyone you know who is a sexual abuse survivor to speak out. Provide your support and comfort in their journey to recovery.

5.   Monitor the media. When you see misinformation, such as so-called "false memories" in the media, write letters, send e-mail, make phone calls--be relentless. Do the same when the media slants stories to promote stereotypes about lesbians, gays, poor, working class people, or single parents. Likewise, praise coverage that serves to end abuse.

6.   Inform public officials and politicians about the issues of child sexual abuse. Demand they include these issues on their agendas. Follow up periodically to determine their use of scapegoats or easy solutions.

7.   Continue to educate yourself and others about the incidence and impact of child sexual abuse, incest and ritual abuse. Keep abreast of the activities of the False Memory Syndrome Foundation and other backlash organizations. Remain current on studies of child abuse and other forms of systemic violence such as racism, sexism and homophobia.

8.   Promote financial support. Raise funds for projects that provide support to survivors and to end child sexual abuse.

9.   Influence organizations working on related issues like domestic violence, rape prevention, youth advocacy, and human rights to include child sexual abuse education and prevention in their agendas.

10.   Become a driving force in your community to promote direct action and advocacy for survivors and against abuse. Become active with other groups fighting oppression and violence.

11.   Encourage sexual abuse survivors to seek professional help with a therapist who specializes in sexual abuse recovery to provide the type of therapy that will assist in healing their wounds. Sexual abuse aftereffects don't go away nor can they be healed with traditional therapy.

Sexual Abuse or Incest Prevention Checklist for Parents and Childcare Workers

___1. Accept the new definition of sexual abuse or incest.

___2. Accept the reality perpetrators can be persons you least expect.

___3. Respect the child's sacred physical boundaries.

___4. Teach and reinforce the child's right to protest uncomfortable or unacceptable touch.

___5. Respect the child's perception of uncomfortable or unacceptable touch.

___6. Respect the child's likes and dislikes.

___7. Avoid using "spanking or hitting" as discipline.

___8. Reinforce the child's right to protest uncomfortable or unwanted touch while doing necessary tasks such as verbally soothing the child and changing the touch.

___9. Accept and practice the guidelines for "good, appropriate" touch.

___10. Intercede when others violate your child's physical boundaries or disregard likes or dislikes.

___11. Teach good body image—"Your body is private, special, beautiful and perfect."

___12. Teach and practice the TELL MOMMY OR DADDY EVERYTHING--NO SECRETS RULE.

___13. Practice appropriate suspicion-check on others' interactions with your child; trust your intuition; heed changes in your child's behavior; investigate behavioral changes and do not stop until you have a resolution.

___14. If in doubt or you have the slightest suspicion your child might be a victim of sexual abuse, seek help from a therapist specializing in sexual abuse recovery and Child Protective Services.

___15. Ask questions, which require "Yes or NO" answers until you are confident you understand what your child is telling you.

___16. Trust your child's perceptions. Children are naturally intuitive and often sense an adult's ulterior motives, although you may not suspect anything.

___17. Trust and act on your intuitiveness or sixth sense.

___18. If you err in evaluating the situation, make the error on the side of your child. The important factor is not that you have avoided offending potential abusers, but that you have protected your child's interest.

HELP AND PREVENTION ORGANIZATIONS

The following organizations are sources of interest in preventing abuse of children. Inclusion of this list does not necessarily indicate an endorsement or recommendation. Use your own judgment when contacting any of these organizations.

One Voice: The National Alliance for Abuse Awareness and its public policy project, The American Coalition for Abuse Awareness (ACAA), P.O. Box 27958, Washington, D.C. 20038-7958; 202-667-1160 or 202-462-4688; fax 202-462-4689; e-mail: OvoiceDC@aol.com or ACAADC@aol.com or on the web: http://www.sover.net/~schwcof/newshead.html
This alliance of survivors, supporters, child advocates, and health care and legal professionals works to educate the public, the media and legislators. Offers a national resource line, legal referrals and information on abuse, trauma, and memory.

Mothers Against Sexual Abuse (MASA), 503 ½ S. Myrtle Ave. #9, Monrovia, CA 91016; 626-305-1986; fax 626-305-5190; or contact MASA via e-mail at: masa@againstsexualabuse.org or on the web: http://againstsexualabuse.org

Offers public education, support for non-offending parents, networking, legislative activism, and a newsletter.

Justice for Children, 412 Main St., Suite 400 Houston, TX 77002; 713-225-4357

Works to protect children when agencies fail to help. Operates a hotline, monitors court proceedings, conducts community forums, and educates elected officials.

The Family Dialogue Project, The Center for Contextual Change, 9239 Gross Point Rd., Skokie, IL 60077; 847-676-4447

Provides services to families seeking mediation as an alternative to legal action in response to allegations of sexual abuse.

The Center for the Prevention of Sexual and Domestic Violence, 936 N 34th Street, Suite 200, Seattle, WA 98103; 206-634-1903; fax 206-634-0115; e-mail: cpsdv@cpsdv.org or on the web: http://www.cpsdv.org

Serves both religious and secular communities, providing excellent literature, books, videos, trainings, conferences, and consultation, and is responsible for groundbreaking work on the relationship between the church and family violence issues.

The Safer Society Foundation (SSFI), P.O. Box 340, Brandon, VT 05733; 802-247-3132; fax 802-247-4233; referral line: 802-247-5141 (M,W,F 1:00—4:30 EST) or on the web: http://www.safersociety.org

This research, advocacy and referral center publishes groundbreaking literature, audio, and videotapes, including the best resources for youthful sex offenders. They maintain a directory of agencies and individuals providing specialized treatment for youthful and adult sex offenders. Also sponsors Stop It Now, which challenges adults to confront abusing behaviors and offers a help line for abusers who want to stop abusing: 888-PREVENT.

SOURCES

1. Araji, S., and D. Finkelhor. "Explanations of Pedophilia: Review of Empirical Research." <u>Bulletin of The American Academy of Psychiatry and the Law</u> 13 (1985): 17-37.
2. Attorney General's Commission on Pornography. <u>Network News</u> 1986, Fall ed.
3. Banning, A. "Mother-Son Incest: Confronting a Prejudice." <u>Child Abuse & Neglect</u> Vol. 13 (4) (1989): 563-570.
4. Bardach, Ann. "Missing Innocence." <u>Vanity Fair</u>. October 29, 1997.
5. Bass, Ellen, and Laura Davis. <u>The Courage to Heal</u>. Harper and Row: New York, NY 1988.
6. Blume, E. Sue. <u>Secret Survivors</u>. Ballantine Books: New York, NY 1991.
7. Briere, J. and J. Conte. "Self-Reported Amnesia for Abuse in Adults Molested as Children." <u>Journal of Traumatic Stress</u> Vol. 6 (1993): 21-31.
8. Brochman, Sue. "Silent Victims: Bringing Male Rape Out of the Closet." <u>The Advocate</u> 582: 38-43.

9. Chasnoff, I.J., et al. "Maternal-Neonatal Incest." American Journal of Orthopsychiatry 56 (4) (1986): 577-580.

10. Conte, Jon R., Steven Wolf, Tim Smith. "What Sexual Offenders Tell Us About Prevention Strategies." Child Abuse & Neglect Vol. 13 (1989): 293-301.

11. Corwin, D. "Early Diagnosis of Child Sexual Abuse: Diminishing the Lasting Effects." in G. Wyatt and G. Powell, eds. The Lasting Effects of Child Sexual Abuse. Sage: Newbury Park, CA 1990.

12. Couric, Katie. Interview with John and Patsy Ramsey. Today Show. NBC. March 20-24, 2000.

13. Dohrenwend, D.P., and Shrout, P.E. "Hassles in the Conceptualization and Measurement of Life Stress Variables." American Psychologist Vol. 40 (7) (1985): 780-785.

14. Donaldson, Donald. "Rape of Males," in Dynes, Wayne, ed. Encyclopedia of Homosexuality. Garland Publications: New York, NY 1990.

15. FBI Uniform Crime Report. Network News 1981.

16. Faller, Kathleen C. "Women Who Sexually Abuse Children." Violence and Victims Vol. 2 (4) (1987): 263-276.

17. Faller, Kathleen C. "Characteristics of a Clinical Sample of Sexually Abused Children: How Boy and Girl Victims Differ." Child Abuse & Neglect Vol. 13 (2) (1989): 281-291.

18. Fantuzzo, J., and Twentyman, Co. "Child Abuse and Psychotherapy Research: Merging Social Concerns

and Empirical Investigation." Professional Psychology and Practice Vol. 17 (5) (1986): 375-380.

19. Feldman-Summers, S. and K. Pope. "The Experience of 'Forgetting' Childhood Abuse: A National Survey of Psychologists." Journal of Consulting and Clinical Psychology Vol.62 (1994): 636-639.

20. Fenickel, Otto, M.D. The Psychoanalytic Theory of Neurosis. W.W. Norton & Company, Inc. 1945: 315.

21. Finkelhor, David. Child Sexual Abuse: New Theory and Research. Free Press: New York, NY 1984.

22. Finkelhor, David and J. Dziuba-Leatherman. "Victimization of Children." American Psychologist Vol. 49:3 (1992): 173-183.

23. Finkelhor, David and Dianna Russell. "Women as Perpetrators: Review of the Evidence." In D. Finkelhor, Child Sexual Abuse New Theory and Research (1984): 171-187 New biblio.

24. Freyd, J.J. "Betrayal Trauma Theory: Traumatic Amnesia as an Adaptive Response to Childhood Abuse." Ethics and Behavior Vol. 4:4 (1994): 307.

25. Gibson, Ian. The English Vice: beating, sex, and shame in Victorian England and after. Duckworth: London, England 1979: 284.

26. Giligun, Jane F. and Teresa M. Connor. "How Perpetrators View Child Sexual Abuse." National Association of Social Workers, Inc. Journal (May 1989): 249 - 251.

27. Ginott, Dr. Haim G. child psychologist. Between Parent and Child. Avon Books: Dresden, TN 1966.

28.   Goldstein-Harte Study 1973: Carter et al, "Use of Pornography in the Criminal and Developmental Histories of Sexual Offenders." 1984.

29.   Goodwin, J., and DiVasto, P. "Female homosexuality: A sequel to mother-daughter incest." In J. M. Goodwin, Sexual Abuse: Incest Victims and Their Families. 2nd ed. Chicago: Year Book Medical Publishers, Inc. 1989: 140-146.

30.   Gore, Tipper. "Hate, Rape and Rap." The Washington Post January 1990.

31.   Greven, Philip. Spare the Child: The Religious Roots of Punishment and the Psychological Impact of Physical Abuse, Vintage Books: New York, NY 1992: 186.

32.   Groth, A. Nicholas. "Understanding Sexual Offense Behavior and Differentiating Among Sexual Abusers." in S. Sgroi Vulnerable Populations. Vol. 2. Lexington Books: Lexington, MA 1989.

33.   Groth, A. Nicholas and Ann Wolbert Burgess. "Male Rape: Offenders and Victims." American Journal of Psychiatry Vol.137 (7) (1980): 806-810.

34.   Harrell, Ken, Craig Lewis and Lynn Allison. "JonBenèt Showed Nine Signs of Sex Abuse." Globe August 1997.

35.   Hay, Louise L. Heal Your Body: The Mental Causes for Physical Illness and the Metaphysical Way to Overcome Them. 4th ed. Hay House: Carson, CA 1994.

36.   Herman, J. and E. Schatzow. "Recovery and Verification of Memories of Childhood Trauma." Psychoanalytic Psychology Vol. 4 (1987): 1-14.

37. Herman, M.D., Judith. Father-Daughter Incest. Harvard University Press: Cambridge, MA 1987.

38. Holden, E.W., S.A.Kosisky, D.J. Willis, and L. Foltz. "Child abuse potential and parenting stress within maltreating families." Paper presented at the 98th annual meeting of the American Psychological Association. Boston, MA. August 10-14, 1990.

39. Hodges, Andrew G., A Mother Gone Bad—the hidden confession of JonBenèt's killer (Village House Publishers, Birmingham, Al., 1998).

40. Holmes, Dr. William C. University of Pennsylvania School of Medicine. Philadelphia Inquirer January 18, 1993.

41. Hunter, Mic. Abused Boys: The Neglected Victims of Sexual Abuse. Lexington Books: Lexington, MA 1990.

42. James, Beverly and Maria Nasjleti. Treating Sexually Abused Children and Their Families. Consulting Psychologists Press: Palo Alto, CA 1983.

43. Janus, PH.D., Sam. The Death of Innocence: How Our Children are Endangered by the New Sexual Freedom. William Morrow & Co., Inc.: Fairfield, NJ 1981.

44. Keating, Kathleen. Hug Therapy 2. CompCare Publishers: Minneapolis, MN 1987.

45. Kempe, Ruth S., C. Henry Kempe. The Common Secret: Sexual Abuse of Children and Adolescents. Harvard University Press: Cambridge, MA 1984.

46. Krug, R.S. "Adult male report of childhood sexual abuse by mothers: Case descriptions, motivations and

long-term consequences." <u>Child Abuse and Neglect</u> Vol. 13(1) (1989): 11-120.

47.　　Krupski, Alli. "Autopsy Confirms Abuse." <u>The Boulder Daily Camera</u> February 15, 1997.

48.　　Krupski, Alli. "JonBenèt's Doctor Rules Out Abuse, Victim Had No History of Sexual Assaults, Pediatrician Says." <u>The Boulder Daily Camera</u> February 16, 1997.

49.　　Lew, Mike. <u>Victims No Longer: Men Recovering from Incest</u>. Perennial Library: New York, NY 1990.

50.　　Loftus, E., S. Polonsky, M. Fullilove. "Memories of Childhood Sexual Abuse." <u>Psychology of Women Quarterly</u> Vol. 18 (1994): 67-84.

51.　　Lukianowicz, N. "Incest, I: Paternal incest; II: Other types of incest." <u>British Journal of Psychiatry</u> Vol. 120 (1972): 301-313.

52.　　Maloney, J.J. "The JonBenèt Autopsy Report: The Complete Autopsy Report." <u>Crime Magazine—An Encyclopedia of Crime</u> December 1998.

53.　　Maloney, J.J. "The Murder of JonBenèt." <u>Crime Magazine—An Encyclopedia of Crime</u> December 1998.

54.　　Matthew, R., J.K. Matthews and K. Speltz. <u>Female Sexual Offenders: An Exploratory Study.</u> The Safer Society Press: Brandon, VT 1989.

55.　　McCarthy, L.M. "Mother-child incest: Characteristics of the offender." <u>Child Welfare.</u> LXV (5) (1986): 447-458.

56.　　Meiselman, K. C. <u>Resolving the Trauma of Incest: Reintegration Therapy with Survivors</u>. Jossey-Bass: San Francisco, CA 1990.

57.   Mendel, Matthew P. The Male Survivor: The Impact of Sexual Abuse. Sage Publications: Newbury Park, CA 1994.

58.   Miller, Alice. Breaking Down the Wall of Silence: The Liberating Experience of Facing Painful Truth. Plenum: New York, NY 1997.

59.   Miller, Alice. Thou Shalt Not Be Aware: Society's Betrayal of the Child. Noonday Press, Imprint of Farrar, Straus & Giroux: Gordonsville, VA 1998.

60.   Miller, Alice, et al. For Your Own Good: Hidden Cruelty in Child-Rearing and the Roots of Violence. Noonday Press, Imprint of Farrar, Straus & Giroux: Gordonsville, VA 1990.

61.   Nicholas, K.B., and S.L. Bieber, "Abusive and supportive parenting behaviors: Differences between mothers and fathers." Paper presented at the 98th Annual Convention of the American Psychological Association, Boston, MA. August 10-14, 1990.

62.   Oliven, J.F. Sexual Hygiene and Pathology. 2nd ed. fully rev. and enl. Lippincott: Philadelphia, PA 1965.

63.   Patton, M.G. Family sexual abuse project: Overview and synthesis of two years of research findings. Paper. May 1, 1987.

64.   Plasket, B. J., "Autopsy Raises More Questions," Longmont FYI—*Daily Times*—Call July 15, 1997.

65.   Plotkin, R.C., S. Azar, C.T. Twentyman, and M.G. Perri. "A critical evaluation of the research methodology employed in the investigation of causative factors of child abuse and neglect." Child Abuse & Neglect Vol. 5(4)(1981): 449-455.

66.   Regensberg, Pam. "Pathologist: JonBenèt Murder Unintentional" Longmont FYI—Daily Times—Call August 13, 1997.

67.   Rowan, E.L., J.B. Rowan, and P. Langelier. "Women who molest children." The Bulletin of the American Academy of Psychiatry and the Law Vol. 18(1) (1981): 79-83.

68.   Russell, Diana. The Secret Trauma: Incest in the Lives of Women and Girls. Basic Books: New York, NY 1986.

69.   Santrock, J.W., R.A. Warshak, and O.L. Elliott, "Social development and parent-child interaction in father-custody and stepmother families." In M.E. Lamb Ed. Nontraditional Families: Parenting and Child Development. Lawrence Erlbaum Associates, Publishers: Hillsdale, NJ 1982: 289-314.

70.   Sawyer, Diane. PrimeTime Live, Interview with Michael Bynum--"The Mystery of JonBenèt Ramsey, Ramsey Family Friend Speaks Out." September 10, 1997.

71.   Scott, George Ryley. The History of Corporal Punishment. AMS Press, Inc.: New York, NY 1986.

72.   Silber, Mimi and Ayala Pines, "Effects of Child Sexual Abuse," Social Work Journal—American Association of Social Workers HV1.S647 360.6273.

73.   Timnick, L. "Children's Abuse Reports Reliable, Most Believe." Los Angeles Times 1985, A1.

74.   U.S. Attorney General. Final Report of the Attorney General's Commission on Pornography. Rutledge Hill Press: Nashville, TN 1986.

75. U.S. Bureau of Justice Statistics. National Crime Survey. Washington, D.C. 1990.

76. U.S. Department of Justice. Source book of Criminal Statistics—Bureau of Justice Statistics. Washington, D.C. 1985.

77. U.S. Department of Justice. Source book of Criminal Statistics—Bureau of Justice Statistics. Washington, D.C. 1992.

78. U.S. Department of Justice. Source book of Criminal Statistics –Bureau of Justice Statistics. Washington, D.C. 1994.

79. U.S. Senate Committee on the Judiciary Hearings before the Subcommittee of Juvenile Justice. "The Effects of Pornography on Children and Women." Testimony of John Rabun, for the National Center for Missing and Exploited Children, September 1984.

80. Vargas, Elizabeth. Interview with Linda Arndt. Good Morning America. ABC. September 13, 1999.

81. Weinberg, K.S. Incest Behavior. Citadel Press, New York, NY 1955.

82. Wildmon, Donald. The Case Against Pornography. Victor Books, Wheaton, IL 1986.

83. Williams, L. "Recall of Childhood Trauma: A Prospective Study of Women's Memories for Child Sexual Abuse." Journal of Consulting and Clinical Psychology Vol. 62 (1994): 1167-1176.

84. Wyatt, Gail E., Gloria Johnson Powell. Lasting Effects of Child Sexual Abuse. Sage Focus Edition, Vol. 100. Sage Publications: Newbury Park, CA 1988.

To The Reader

The author welcomes your comments and reactions, or the sharing of personal experiences that relate to your reading of *If I'd Only Known… Sexual Abuse in or out of the Family: A Guide to Prevention.* To share your thoughts or to contact Ms. Neddermeyer for professional purposes, write to: Genesis Consultants, Inc. P.O. Box 1006, Maplewood, NJ 07040 or Telephone: 973-762-4854, e-mail address: DorothyNed@aol.com or visit the website at http://www.Gen-Assist.com.

About The Author

Dorothy M. Neddermeyer is a psychotherapist who specializes in sexual abuse, incest and physical abuse survivor recovery. She is: an author, lecturer and trainer on a variety of issues; a New York state certified social worker; a New Jersey licensed clinical social worker; a member of the National Association of Social Workers, a Diplomat of the National Board of Certified Clinical Hypnotherapists, and is listed in Who's Who in American Women, 2000 edition.

Endorsements

"Dorothy Neddermeyer's book places emphasis on the extraordinary need for empathy in the prevention of sexual and physical abuse. Her work demonstrates her vast experience with the complexity of the problems and recognition associated with abuse, and the necessity for every parent to be aware of the approaches and measures needed to evaluate our children and their needs."

> – Frederick Kahn, M.D., Psychiatrist Private Practice, Paramus, NJ

"… a straight-to-the-point, informative resource for every parent, teen, or adult responsible for the safety and well-being of a child. Ms. Neddermeyer is to be commended for the courageous manner in which she has told the traumatic story of sexual abuse – a story that will help millions to accept, perhaps for the first time ever, that they are not alone and that it wasn't "their fault" … she empowers her readers with the practical resources needed to prevent and interrupt this vicious assault on America's children."

> -- Pamela L. Blyth, Healthcare Management Consultant and Trainer

"As the parent of three children [two boys and a girl] and therapist, I am aware of the delicate balance parents walk to protect, but not over protect a child from harm. Because I am a sexual abuse survivor, by a family member, I am particularly attuned to this issue. Dorothy Neddermeyer addresses this highly charged topic without vilifying the perpetrator while holding him or her totally responsible for this crime. Another strong point of this book lies in Ms. Neddermeyer's ability to relate clinical information and research in a consistently humanistic and compassionate manner. She outlines clear, concise techniques to protect children at all ages from this horrible crime. I highly recommend this book to anyone who has child care responsibility."

– Terry J. Howell, M.A., Counseling Psychologist

"Dorothy Neddermeyer offers an excellent guide to the causes and results of sexual abuse. She is adept at getting into the minds of both the abused and the abuser, and helps us understand clearly the long-term ramifications of childhood trauma. An acute cultural observer, the author also critiques a society that tacitly overlooks the problem. Most important Ms. Neddermeyer offers practical ways for the reader to protect children against America's greatest unacknowledged scourge."

-- Rev. Dr. Robert L. Gram, Senior Minister, Wyckoff Reformed Church, Wyckoff, NJ